HUMAN DEVELOPMENT BOOKS:
A SERIES IN APPLIED BEHAVIORAL SCIENCE

Joseph and Laurie Braga, *general editors*

HUMAN DEVELOPMENT BOOKS is a series designed to bridge the gap between research and theory in the behavioral sciences and practical application by readers. Each book in the series deals with an issue important to the growth and development of human beings, as individuals and in interaction with one another. At a time when the pressures and complexities of the world are making increased demands on people's ability to cope, there is a need for tools that can help individuals take a more active role in solving their own problems and in living life more fully. Such information is not easily found or read by those without previous experience or familiarity with the vocabulary of a particular behavioral field. The books in this series were designed and executed to meet that purpose.

MARGARET HELLIE HUYCK is in the Department of Psychology at the Illinois Institute of Technology, in Chicago.

BOOKS IN THE SERIES

Growing with Children, by Joseph and Laurie Braga
Growing Older, by Margaret Hellie Huyck
Learning and Growing: A Guide to Child Development, by Joseph and Laurie Braga (*in production*)
Death: The Final Stage of Growth, by Elisabeth Kübler-Ross (*in production*)
Culture and Human Development, by Ashley Montagu (*in production*)

growing
older

what you need to know
about aging

margaret hellie huyck

104154

A SPECTRUM BOOK

prentice-hall, inc., englewood cliffs, new jersey

Library of Congress Cataloging in Publication Data

HUYCK, MARGARET HELLIE.
 Growing older.

 (Human development books) (A Spectrum Book)
 Bibliography: p.
 1. Aging. 2. Middle age. 3. Old age. I. Title.
HQ1064.U5H88   301.43′5   74–8061
 ISBN 0–13–367771–0
 ISBN 0–13–367763–X (pbk.)

© 1974 BY MARGARET HELLIE HUYCK

A SPECTRUM BOOK

2 3 4 5 6 7 8 9 10

Printed in the United States of America

PRENTICE-HALL INTERNATIONAL, INC. (LONDON)
PRENTICE-HALL OF AUSTRALIA PTY., LTD. (SYDNEY)
PRENTICE-HALL OF CANADA, LTD. (TORONTO)
PRENTICE-HALL OF INDIA PRIVATE LIMITED (NEW DELHI)
PRENTICE-HALL OF JAPAN, INC. (TOKYO)

contents

foreword

Aging is an issue in human development that is shared by all of us. We will all become older, but we will not all be affected by the aging process in the same way. Whether you will simply age as the years pass or will *grow* older is the focus of this volume. Because the physical changes that accompany the aging process are viewed in negative ways, aging is often seen as signalling deterioration rather than as a further development. Physical changes are inevitable; but their impact on your functioning is relative to your ability to accommodate those changes. (For example, as you grow older, your body burns up calories at a slower rate, so you need less food; if you don't want to gain weight, you must cut your food intake and increase your level of activity). To base our total view of aging on the physical aspects of the process, however, is to miss the most important parts of growing older.

Whereas our physical being is at its prime in the early part of our lives, our psychological and intellectual beings may continue to grow throughout our entire life span. It is true that many people stop growing in any way at an early age, but the models of highly creative and productive people give us a vision of what can be. Margaret Hellie Huyck points out repeatedly, in relation to physical, sexual, intellectual, and psychological functioning, that there is one rule that seems to be consistently true: *Use it or lose it*. Evidence is accumulating that indicates you are much more in control of how you age than is popularly believed. You need not accept the view of aging as deterioration; if you choose to continue to grow and develop as you grow older, you will very likely be able to do so.

Dr. Huyck offers us a view of the aging process that reflects current research and theory in the various aspects of gerontology. She approaches the topic of *growing older* from the perspective of things you should be aware of in order to deal more effectively with the problems and issues related to aging. And she presents many angles on the subject so that you may better understand the interaction of such factors as culture, economics, social expectations and norms—as well as the biological changes that affect how a person ages. Through confronting the issues, problems, and myths of aging, the author attempts to lead readers to explore the ways in which they can ensure that their aging can be a continuation of their development as persons.

Living, at whatever age you are, should be a search for self—the discovery and enhancement of those things that are most truly and profoundly you. When this is true, there is no age at which it is too late to grow. Dr. Huyck pays particular attention to the role expectations and norms (things you are or are not supposed to do because you belong to a certain age group, sex, class, and so on) that define and confine people, keeping them from growing. For example, she points out in Chapter 2 that an "old lady" might be inhibited in her desire to study Chinese by the fact that young people do not expect older people to continue to learn.

The impact of "agism" in our society is individually and socially devastating. In a society in which built-in obsolescence is the accepted rule, people are similarly valued less and excluded from participation in the society as they become older. Attitudes toward the old, both by the young and consequently by the old themselves, are negative and damaging to an aging person's feelings about himself. In addition, as a society, we are losing some of our most basic human values in our rejection of the elderly.

The word elderly is derived from *elder,* a term of respect in other times, and today in some societies. Although it is not automatically a consequence of growing older, wisdom and long-term perspective are usually associated with older members of a social group. An understanding of the long-range consequences of various courses of action is more readily available to those who have lived long enough to see the results of different decisions. The sense of continuity of past with present and future, so important in understanding life's meaning, is possible only through communication between old and young. Many human skills and crafts, once passed through generations, have been replaced by machines, and the last vestiges of these parts of human culture are dying off with the oldest members of our society.

It is important to all of us to begin to change our negative attitudes about aging. The superficial qualities that we must relinquish as the years make their imprint are not nearly as valuable as the growth as persons that we can accomplish if we view growing older as a necessary component of the total process of growth and development. We owe it to ourselves and to our elders to restore the dignity to being old, so that we may live all of our years as fully as possible. Will you accept being put out to pasture when society, family, and friends tell you that you are no longer young? Or will you demand to continue living as long as you are alive?

We join with Margaret Hellie Huyck in hoping that the facts and interpretations provided in this volume will help you deal more effectively with the problems and issues related to aging. Through knowledge and understanding of the developmental process and of the issues you are likely to face, you should be able to anticipate and cope better with those issues as they affect you personally.

JOSEPH L. BRAGA
LAURIE D. BRAGA
General Editors

preface

Many adults in our society can expect to live a long life—perhaps a century. Because this is a relatively recent expectation, we are not well prepared as individuals or as a society to understand or cope with old age. We can expect our parents to live longer, and this puts new demands on our abilities to deal with changes in their behavior. We want to plan for our own long lives, and we may be unhappy with the model of aging provided by our parents. We may wonder whether old age must be so full of decline and despair. We may wish to deny its existence and avoid confronting our own aging. But *now* is when we must begin planning for our old age—while we are *growing older;* we cannot wait until we've *grown old.*

This book can be a tool in preparing for a long, satisfying life. One of the things it reveals is that most of the behaviors and characteristics of the old are not inevitable—and they may be reversible. Many of the decreases in functioning observed among the elderly are not so much related to age as to the situations in which the elderly find themselves.

To prepare for one's own old age, it is important to understand which issues are likely to be important in the second half of life. Issues are not necessarily problems, but they must be dealt with. For example, it is predictable that the loss of people close to one will be an issue, and it *could* be a problem, but there *are* ways to deal with it. The focus of this book will be on likely issues in various areas, and ways in which it may be possible to cope with them.

This book stresses the variety of patterns of successful aging. There is no magic formula for success and happiness in old age. Happy older adults are quite different from each other, as well as different from the less happy. Furthermore, happy older adults seem to have been happy in middle age—and probably in young adulthood.

The central point emerging from the study of aging is that we take ourselves with us as we grow older. We arrange, perceive, and interpret life events in quite distinctive ways, and the ways in which we do this seem to remain the same as we grow older. How we live now, what our attitudes are toward living, growing, and aging, will be the most influential factors in determining how we age.

The stereotypes of aging in our culture are negative—and often untrue. Realistic problems do exist, but they may be overemphasized. Most of them can be resolved if we put a high social priority on doing so. For example, a current "reality" of old age is a reduced standard of living, accompanied by a poorer self-concept; these result from a cultural system in which income is related to current productivity and the value of the elderly is low. Positive change in the "facts" will occur when we alter the social conditions which make aging an undesirable process.

The aging process affects not only individuals but the whole society. The birth rate is declining, and survival to old age is increasingly common. Older adults will continue to make up a growing proportion of the population. This reality has already made more demands for social programs to meet the needs of older Americans. What will our society be like if 20 percent (instead of 4 percent in 1900 and 10 percent now) of the population is over 65? We must start preparing for this eventuality now.

This book has had many helpers. Bernice Neugarten and others at the University of Chicago introduced me to the study of adult development, and I have benefited from Dr. Neugarten's guidance for many years. I appreciate the willingness of all the authors and publishers whose work is contained herein to extend permission to reprint their material as illustrations of various points about aging. The editors for this series, Laurie and Joe Braga, have excellent ideas and I have benefited from their helpful suggestions. Mariette Vandendorpe has collaborated on the project from the beginning, found many of the literary selections, and performed administrative tasks admirably.

The guiding light is, as always, my husband Tom—I enjoy growing older with him.

MARGARET HELLIE HUYCK

1

introduction: how old are you?

What do you feel when you think about growing older? Do you feel frightened and uneasy? How do you feel about old people? Do they seem slow, poor, useless, and friendless? Perhaps old people call up images of walking canes, hospital beds, medicinal smells, and final surrender to death. How did you react to the last old person you confronted? Were you silent and embarrassed, not sure how to react? Did you try to avoid contact, or feel pity? Or perhaps you felt awed at the sheer ability to survive. What age do you consider old—Forty? Sixty? Eighty? Are you old when you can't learn anything new? When you no longer earn money for your work? When no one willingly looks upon you? When you *feel* old?

What does it mean to grow older? Perhaps the sentiments above reflect some of your feelings. Younger people in our society often view aging only as loss. However, you may value old age for gains in wisdom and life experience, sharing the old Chinese philosophy of Confucius:

At 15, I applied myself to the study of wisdom.
At 30, I grew strong in it.
At 40, I no longer had doubt.
At 50, there was nothing on earth that could shake me.
At 70, I could follow the dictate of my heart without disobeying moral law.

This book is meant to explore both the gains and the realistic losses involved in growing older.

We all care about aging because we are all growing older. We can expect many changes even after we have "grown up," and we will grow older before we become old.

We all probably *will* become old. In Biblical times, the life expectancy was twenty-seven or thirty-five; now it is approximately seventy-five years for women and seventy-two for men. This means that those who are in their twenties now can expect to live a half-century more; those in their forties now still have three or four decades to plan for. Try to imagine what you will be doing in twenty years . . . in forty years. How will you feel about yourself then? Will you be as eager to explore the world as you are now? Will you concentrate more on satisfying your own dreams? Will you feel depressed that your youth has faded slowly away?

Our future will be longer than any previous generation's, and this fact makes it essential that we gain insight into the aging process before we become old. Some biologists predict that the average life expectancy will reach 100 before the end of this century. Few of us are now prepared for ten decades of life; almost all the social preparation focuses on the first three decades of learning, working, marrying, and child-rearing.

This book will set out the normal developmental issues of adulthood, to interpret some of the changes we can all expect to encounter as we grow older. Change is inevitable, but it is also threatening. This book will describe both the positive and negative aspects of predictable changes, and suggest what can be done to lessen the negative aspects. It is possible to compensate for many of the losses of aging—but only if we know the possibilities and feel free to demand the same help we would expect to receive as young persons.

A developmental issue is not necessarily a crisis. Many of us think now in terms of the "crisis of old age," since much of the mass media describe it in those terms. Aging may bring to mind the "crisis of retirement," the "crisis of the empty nest," or the "crisis of the menopause." However, withdrawing from full-time paid work, raising children to adulthood, and the gradual ending of menstrual flow in women are all quite normal, predictable occurrences.

There are developmental "issues" at different stages of anyone's life. Adjusting to new parenthood is an issue for young adults; adjusting to grandparenthood is a task for older adults. Because we share a common biology and a common culture, there are regularities in the issues or "tasks" which everybody meets as they grow older.

The concept of "age" can have different meanings. Probably one's first response to the question "How old are you?" is one's chronological age—how many years since one's birth. This is only one measure of age. The unit of chronological age is the same for all people, so ages are easily compared and ranked; it is very clear when one becomes the *next* age (on one's birthday); and, during childhood, chronological age is a fairly good predictor of developmental level. Thus, most three-year-olds can walk but few can read; and most nine-year-old girls in our culture are concerned with mastering academic and athletic skills, while sixteen-year-olds are more concerned with social skills. However, even by the time of adolescence, chronological age may not be a very good "predictor," if we want to know who will do fifty pushups or take over the family laundry. As time passes, chronological age becomes increasingly less useful as an index for understanding and predicting behavior. Persons attending a high-school twentieth-year reunion will probably find that they are less alike than they were as adolescents. Different life experiences will make that same group at age seventy even more diverse.

Another measure is biological age; this means how well the physical organism functions. If we wished to predict which people over the chronological age of fifty could survive a heart transplant or maintain an independent household, biological age would have to be assessed.

There are also social time clocks by which to measure the passing of time. The twenty-year-old who is married and a parent is usually seen by others and by himself as "older" (or more "mature") than the twenty-year-old who is in college, living with parents, and dating. A seventy-year-old who is working full time and lives with a spouse in their own home is seen as "younger" than the seventy-year-old in a nursing home.

It is useful to have a measure of age that reflects psychological aspects of behavior. Intellectual age is a common measurement during childhood, and if we are concerned about the ability to learn or the amount already learned during adulthood, we may wish to assess "mental age" in adults. Or, recognizing the emerging evidence that personality processes may undergo normal developmental changes during adulthood, we can assess psychological age in terms of nearness to typical perspectives and concerns of "middle-aged" or "old" persons.

Finally, the best measure of psychological age may be the question "How old do you feel?" Responses to this question, in fact, can tell us quite accurately how a person will behave. A person who reports *feeling* old (regardless of chronological age, social age, and often even biological age) is likely to behave more in accordance with our stereotypes of the old.

THE "STAGES"
OF DEVELOPMENT

In attempting to identify various stages in one's own development one would probably set aside at least three: childhood, adulthood, and old age, since all societies recognize these stages. Perhaps some might also distinguish many stages in early development—infancy, toddlerhood, early childhood, school-age or middle childhood, preadolescence, early adolescence, late adolescence, youth, young adulthood. One might be more uncertain about how to identify stages in adulthood, or what to call them.

A *stage* implies that individuals in that stage are at a similar developmental level, and that they can be identified by common abilities, behavior, or problems. One of the most famous word pictures of the seven ages of man was written by William Shakespeare. His images of old age are particularly frightening, emphasizing the lacks and the losses.

THE SEVEN AGES OF MAN

All the world's a stage.
And all the men and women merely players.
They have their exists and their entrances.
And one man in his time plays many parts.
His acts being seven ages. At first, the infant,
Mewing and puking in the nurse's arms.
Then the whining schoolboy, with his satchel
And shining morning face, creeping like a snail
Unwillingly to school. And then the lover,
Sighing like a furnace, with a woeful ballad
Made to his mistress' eyebrow. Then a soldier,
Full of strange oaths and bearded like the pard,
Jealous in honour, sudden and quick in quarrel,
Seeking the bubbly reputation
Even in the cannon's mouth. And then the justice,
In fair round belly with good capon lin'd,
With eyes severe and beard of formal cut,
Full of wise saws and modern instances;
And so he plays his part. The sixth age shifts

Into the lean and slipper'd pantaloon,
With spectacles on nose and pouch on side;
His youthful hose, well sav'd, a world too wide
For his shrunk shank, and his big manly voice,
Turning again toward childish trebel, pipes
And whistles in his sound. Last scene of all,
That ends this strange eventful History,
Is second childishness and mere oblivion,
Sans teeth, sans eyes, sans taste, sans everything.[1]

Shakespeare presented old age as an inglorious end to a generally ridiculous life. Perhaps his description was more accurate in the days before Medicare, dentures, eyeglasses, and Social Security.

The psychologist Erik Erikson[2] sees the eight stages of life as defined by the special challenges to be met in each stage. One may meet the challenges well or poorly, and the way one resolves the issues at one stage will affect one's life in the next stages. The earlier childhood challenges have to do with establishing a sense of trust in the world and in one's own abilities. The adolescent task is to develop a firm sense of identity, an answer to the question "Who am I?" Erikson discusses three successive issues in adulthood. Establishing a sense of intimacy and overcoming a sense of isolation is usually a young-adult task—but may become an issue again if one loses one's partner later on. "Generativity" concerns are the next issue; these involve concern for the survival and welfare of the coming generations and is typically reflected in having children and raising them. Adults may instead indulge themselves and suffer a sense of "stagnation." The final issue in Erikson's scheme is to develop a sense of ego integrity. Integrity is the outcome of a mentally healthy life. Erikson expresses it best.

INTEGRITY VS. DESPAIR
AND DISGUST

Only he who in some way has taken care of things and people and has adapted himself to the triumphs and disappointments of being, by necessity, the originator of others and the generator of things and

---

[1] *As You Like It* (II, vii, 139–66).
[2] Read especially "The Eight Stages of Man in Erik Erikson," *Childhood and Society* (New York: W. W. Norton, 1963).

ideas—only he may gradually grow the fruit of the seven stages. I know no better word for it than *integrity*. Lacking a clear definition, I shall point to a few attributes of this state of mind. It is the acceptance of one's own and only life cycle and of the people who have become significant to it as something that had to be and that, by necessity, permitted of no substitutions. It thus means a new and different love of one's parents, free of the wish that they should have been different, and an acceptance of the fact that one's life is one's own responsibility. It is a sense of comradeship with men and women of distant times and of different pursuits, who have created orders and objects and sayings conveying human dignity and love. Although aware of the relativity of all the various life styles which have given meaning to human striving, the possessor of integrity is ready to defend the dignity of his own life style against all physical and economic threats. For he knows that an individual life is the accidental coincidence of but one life cycle with but one segment of history; and that for him all human integrity stands and falls with the one style of integrity of which he partakes.[3]

The "stage" concept is a useful way of describing some of the common themes in development. However, all behavior and needs cannot usefully be associated with certain stages. There are needs that cut across all ages and stages: e.g., the needs to be safe from harm, to feel loved and accepted, and to feel competent. These become "issues" and problems when they are not being met, regardless of age.

Many sources of information are useful in the study of aging. Autobiography, fiction, and poetry provide insights. Personal observations and clinical "case study" reports give illustrations of common themes and examples of individual variability. Systematic research investigations are important because this is how assumptions and speculations about aging can be tested. It is really only through wide-scale, scientific study that we can answer such questions as: Is there a male menopause? Does intelligence decline with age? Does the status of the elderly get worse when there are more of them in a society? Are older people who are working happier than those who are retired? How does a marriage change over fifty years? How is the experience of aging different for men and women?

Systematic investigations of developmental issues are very difficult.

3 Erik Erikson, "Growth and Crises of the Healthy Personality," *Psychological Issues*, I, 1959, p. 98.

In order to measure changes over long periods of time (fifty years at least), researchers must know how to measure change.

Suppose we decide to gather information next month on representative samples of individuals who are twenty, thirty, forty, fifty, sixty, seventy, eighty and ninety years old. If we give each one the same intelligence test, we can compare the results as soon as the data are collected. From this procedure, we can see if fifty-year-olds score higher or lower than twenty-year-olds in IQ. By plotting the results on a graph we can obtain an "age curve" for that behavior. This way of studying age changes is called the *cross-sectional* method, because the researcher takes a cross section of all the ages he wants to study and collects the data at one time. The researcher then treats his data *as if* it represented the predictable course for any individual; he assumes that the thirty-year-olds tested next month would show IQ scores similar to those of the seventy-year-olds if the younger group was retested forty years later.

However, they may not. While inferring individual curves from cross-sectional data is a reasonable way to begin to examine age changes, this method also measures cultural change. People with more formal education have higher IQ test scores. Older people today have had less formal education than younger people, and *this* may well account for much of the "decline" in IQ scores with increased age. A *longitudinal* method of study retests the *same* group of individuals at several different times, and charts the changes over time. Although not free from cultural effects either, the longitudinal method is probably the best one for determining the intrinsic or "natural" effects of aging. If researchers can demonstrate consistent changes with age in longitudinal studies in many cultures, then we can begin to talk about intrinsic, inevitable effects of advancing age. We have at this time virtually no evidence meeting these rigorous specifications. Our comments about aging will remain speculations and reasonable hypotheses until considerably more research is completed.

Having given this warning, I will not dwell on the lack of proof for the comments that follow in this book. The conclusions drawn seem the most reasonable ones at this time. Future research may change some of the conclusions presented here, since the systematic study of aging is a very new field.

However, systematic research over the past two decades reveals certain patterns in the process of aging. We can use this information to anticipate the future.

2

social expectations:
act your age!

If one were told that an old maiden lady was coming to dinner, what images would come to mind? One might drag out the rocking chair, dust off some antique records, and worry about conversing with a person so near the grave. In doing this, one would be acting on *stereotypes:* commonly accepted beliefs about the ways individuals who possess certain characteristics (age, color, sex, accent) will behave. Actually, this old lady might prefer the beanbag chair and blues music, and she may be studying Chinese and pollution control. In acting on stereotypes, one may miss reality.

In addition to stereotypes, all cultures have *age norms:* expectations about what is desirable behavior at any given age. There are also norms specific to sex, and, in some cultures, to ethnicity (e.g., Irish, Black, Jew) and social class. The feelings we have about ourselves depend in part on meeting the expectations of our culture. Because most people want the rewards that come with conforming to norms, these norms act as a system of social control. Thus, our behavior is shaped by the expectations others hold for us and that we accept for ourselves.

Norms that are based on age, sex, and ethnicity are particularly important because they depend on characteristics we can do nothing about. They are what sociologists have termed "ascribed characteristics," because they are inherent at birth and are not subject to change. While age is an "ascribed characteristic," it does change—in a predictable, universal direction. (Thus, while we all might prefer to meet the norms of a twenty-five-year-old forever, we too will move gradually into the ranks of middle age and old age.) On the other hand, some characteristics are "achieved" because they are open to change by choice. For example, one may change one's occupation; if someone does not want to meet the norms and expectations of a professor, he or she may become a plumber.

Culturally accepted norms and stereotypes can lead to a self-fulfilling prophesy—because we expect something to be a certain way, it turns out that way. For example, if the age norms are that our old lady is "too old" to learn Chinese, others may refuse to teach her or react with amazement if she tries. If she fully accepted the norms, she might not even try, or would give up easily because success was not expected.

A *social role* is a useful way to see how norms shape behavior. A social role includes expected behavior, privileges, and responsibilities. Wife, husband, worker, clerk, grandmother, hooker, host, and student are all social roles. We all grew up learning how to enact a variety of roles; as we grow older our roles change. The roles we enact affect the experiences we have. If someone is a student, others will expect him to read books, attend classes, and demonstrate his learning; if he does these things, he will feel good about himself. Some roles have many, clearly defined expectations, sometimes formalized in law (such as husband and wife); other roles have minimal requirements or very vague ones.

It is well established that social stereotypes based on sex exist in our culture (and all others), and that there are "social roles" of man and woman. It is important to understand how our behavior is affected by sex role stereotypes because these mean that the aging process is a different experience for men and for women.

What stereotypes and social roles exist for age? Perhaps some of us have felt pressured by friends and relatives to get married ("Haven't you found anyone *yet?*"), or have a child ("before you're too old"), or get a job promotion. In our culture, the twenties are seen as a "good time" to settle on a mate and start a career. To be a young man involves a certain set of expectations—a social role.

Think about a seventy-year-old man . . . should he drive a red convertible? Start writing his memoirs? Court a forty-year-old woman? What about a fifty-year-old woman . . . should she wear a bikini to the beach? Start training to be a computer programmer? Have an affair with a twenty-five-year-old man? Many persons may well have feelings about the appropriateness of these behaviors, and those who do may be reflecting age norms.

The norms for older adults seem to be less clearly defined than those for young adults. There is no clearly defined social role of "senior citizen." As one might imagine, this can be anxiety-provoking to some individuals if they wish clear-cut expectations to follow. Other individuals welcome the personal freedom possible when social norms are minimal.

Popular stereotypes of old people contain both positive and negative aspects—and younger people are generally much more pessimistic about aging than are the elderly. Social class affects perceptions of different stages of adulthood. Middle-class people tend to see young adulthood as a period of exploration, middle age as bringing control, mastery, and responsibility, and a short old age involving leisure, relaxation, and security. Lower-class people see a short middle age, and a long old age of progressive physical decline, senility, and full retirement.[1] Thus, views of aging and old people are influenced by our position in society.

The research summarized below by Bernice L. Neugarten indicates that subgroups in our society share a common set of norms for age and sex, and that these norms influence individual behavior.

Age Norms

Bernice L. Neugarten

We began by asking, What is the psychological significance of a given chronological age? How does the person mark off and evaluate the passage of time? It is clear that people do not evaluate lifetime merely by reckoning the number of years since their birth. The statement, "I am 50 years old" has little significance; but, rather, "I am 50 years old and farther ahead than I expected to be," or "farther behind than

[1] Bernice Neugarten and W. A. Peterson. "A Study of the American Age-Grade System," *Proceedings*, 4th Congress of the International Association of Gerontology, Bolzano, Italy, pp. 1–6.

———Edited from "Personality and the Aging Process," by Bernice L. Neugarten, the 1971 Robert W. Kleemeier Award Lecture delivered at the 24th Annual Meeting of the Gerontological Society, and printed in *The Gerontologist*, Spring, 1972, pp. 9–15. Reprinted by permission of the author and The Gerontological Society.

other men in the same line of work." In such everyday phrases, the individual gives content and meaning to the passage of time, and he refers to an implicit normative system in comparing himself to others.

To understand this normative system we undertook some exploratory studies of age status, age norms, and age expectations, perceiving them as forming a cultural context against which to view the person's evaluation of lifetime. First we studied the extent to which there was consensus regarding age norms. We recognized that in a complex modern society, there are multiple systems of age status that characterize different institutions and that changes in age roles are not synchronous. (For example, in the political institutions of this society, a man is adult at 18 when he can vote; but in the family he is adult when he marries and becomes a parent, usually several years later than 18.) We asked if, nevertheless, there were an age-status system common to the society as a whole.

We interviewed a representative sample of 600 middle-aged and older people and found widespread agreement in response to questions like these:

> What would you call the periods of life that people go through after they are grown up? At what age does each period begin for most people? What are the important changes from one period to the next?

We found that middle-aged people perceived adulthood as composed of four different life periods, each with its characteristic pattern of personal and social behavior: young adulthood, maturity, middle age, and old age. Progression from one period to the next was described along one of five dimensions: events in the occupational career; events of the family cycle; changes in health; changes in psychological attributes (e.g., "middle age is when you become mellow"); and/or changes in social responsibilities (e.g., "old age is when you let the other fellow do the worrying").

From these data it was possible to delineate the first gross outline of a system of age expectations that encompasses various areas of adult life. There appeared to be a set of social age definitions that provided a frame of reference by which the experiences of adult life were perceived as orderly and rhythmical. Although perceptions varied by sex and by social class (e.g., old age begins earlier in the perceptions of working-class than in middle-class people) there was nevertheless a striking degree of consensus.

We next asked questions regarding age-appropriate and age-linked behaviors:

> What do you think the best age for a man to marry? to hold his top job? for a woman to become a grandmother? What age comes to your mind when you think of a young man? an old man? When a man has the most responsibilities?

There was widespread consensus, also, in responses to items such as these that pertained to work, to family, and to other areas of life. To illustrate, most middle-class men and women agreed that the best age for a man to marry was from 20 to 25; most men should be settled in a career by 24 to 26; they should hold their top jobs by 40; be ready to retire by 60 to 65; and so on. There appears, then, to be a prescriptive timetable for the ordering of major events in the individual's lifeline. Age expectations seemed more clearly focused—that is, consensus was greatest—for the period of young adulthood, as if the normative system bears more heavily upon individuals as they move into adulthood than when they move into middle or old age. There was greater consensus with regard to age-appropriate behavior for women than for men, and again, consistent variation by social class. The higher the social class, the later the ages associated with all major life events.

We moved next to asking, How does this system of age-norms function? How is it demonstrated in the lives of people? We therefore asked respondents about actual occurrences: how old were they when they left their parents' home? married? had their first full-time job? their first child? grandchild? top job? retired? We found that the similarities between occurrences and norms were striking. In short, the actual timing of major life events, especially in young adulthood, tends to adhere to the prescriptive timetable. The normative system seems to function as a system of social control—as prods and brakes upon behavior. In other words, most people do things when they think they "should" do them; and they seem to follow a social clock that becomes internalized so that they can tell an interviewer readily enough if they are late, early, or on time with regard to major life events; and with regard to various types of achievement.

We repeated these studies with other groups of respondents: with a group of young married men and women, all around age 25, who lived in a small midwestern city; with a group aged 70 to 80 who lived in a small New England community; with a sample of middle-class blacks who lived in a medium-sized midwestern city. Although some variations appeared, the same general patterns emerged in each set of data, indicating considerable consensus about these types of age norms and age expectations.

We also explored related questions. How do people learn the norms? What are the sanctions in the system, the types of social approval and disapproval that operate to keep people on time? How, in short, does this normative system operate as social control? We have various data showing that age deviancy is always of psychological significance to the individual, but we have not yet obtained good data on how the social mechanisms operate.

Given our conviction that age norms and age expectations constitute a system of social control, we worked out a method for pursuing the question, Do people vary in the degree of constraint they perceive with regard to those norms? We asked such questions as:

> Would you approve of a woman who wears a two-piece bathing suit to the beach when she is 18? when she's 35? 55?
>
> What about a woman who decides to have another child at 40? at 35? at 30?
>
> What about a couple who move across country to live near their married children when they are 40? 55? 75?

We found that middle-aged and old people see greater constraints in the age-norm system than do the young. They seem to have learned that age and age-appropriateness are reasonable criteria by which to evaluate behavior; that to be off-time with regard to major life events brings with it negative consequences. In the young there is a certain denial that age is a valid dimension by which to judge behavior.

We have begun to explore the psychological correlates of age-deviancy. For instance, in two studies of Army officers (the U.S. Army is a clearly age-graded set of occupations, where the investigator can create an objective measure of who is on-time and who is off-time) it could be demonstrated that being off-time with regard to career has psychological and social accompaniments. On-time and off-time men differed not only with regard to evaluations of their careers, but also with regard to self-esteem, mobility aspirations, anticipated adjustment to retirement, perception of status in the civilian community, and degree of social integration in the community.*

* The symbol ↰ designates the end of a selection.

DOUBLE STANDARD?

Some observers have perceived a "double standard of aging," with different expectations of men than of women; this double standard is reminiscent of the double standard of sexual behavior for young men and women—men did and nice girls didn't. In support of this contention, they cite the mass-media advertising, in which the women who are presented as desirable to men are young and beautiful, the myriads of products offered women to help deny physical aging, and clothing designed for young rather than mature female figures. Femininity is equated with reproductive ability or sex appeal. Men, on the other hand, are presented as desirable if potent, and potency is equated with power and control. Generally, men increase in power (social, not physical) at least through middle age. Thus, women lose femininity and value as they age, while men enhance their masculinity as they grow older.

Imagine your response to a middle-aged woman dating a younger man. If you feel disgust, disbelief, embarrassment, or pity, your reaction is probably typical in our culture. However, your response to seeing an older man teamed romantically with a woman young enough to be his daughter might well be one of approval, acceptance, or even envy. That is a double standard—and an unfortunate one now being challenged. For one thing, sex research makes it clear that men reach their peak in the late teens, while women are most responsive and interested in their thirties and forties. Sexually, an older women teamed with a young man may be a better match. Women are refusing to consider themselves romantically obsolete at middle age. And, if women would marry men younger than they (rather than older), they would be less likely to have a long widowhood. The double standard is not logical.

The fact of the double standard may put the older woman in a position where she is worse off; it is not clear, however, that women necessarily have a "harder time" growing older than do men. It may be more accurate, and helpful, to understand that the issues faced and the resources available may be different for men and women as long as sex provides a social role.

AGISM, SEXISM, AND RACISM

What about other consequences of stereotyped expectations? The psychological "cost" may be fairly great for strict adherence to sex and age norms; other research has fully documented the emotional "cost" of negative stereotypes associated with race. We can also look at more tangible costs: income. The price of being female or Black has been repeatedly demonstrated in recent years; the economic costs of being the "wrong" age have been less fully explored.

The relative effects of agism, sexism, and racism were explored in a study by Palmore and Manton.[2] They wanted to know "Which is stronger in our society: race, sex, or age inequality?" Racism, sexism, and agism were defined as

> attitudes and behaviors, either individual or institutional, which discriminate against a person because of his or her race, sex, or age. The concept of institutional or structural discrimination is becoming more important as it becomes apparent that much inequality results from the policies and procedures of key institutions in our society (such as compulsory retirement) rather than from consciously biased actions of prejudiced individuals. Indeed, institutional discrimination may well be the primary link between personal ideology and these group inequalities. Institutional discrimination may also change more slowly because it is often associated with basic social values and norms (the neighborhood school, women's place is in the home, retirement at 65).

One of the conclusions from the Palmore and Manton study was that agism "costs" more than racism or sexism. They found that each of the variables were costly: Blacks earn less than whites, women earn less than men, and older people earn less than younger. These "liabilities" are additive: the poorest are old Black women; the best paid are younger white males.

Palmore and Manton looked at these costs over several years and concluded that racial inequalities declined, sex inequalities were essentially unchanged, and age inequalities were getting worse. This suggests that agism may indeed be the "sleeper issue" as older people demand a reasonable income.

[2] Erdman Palmore and Kenneth Manton, "Agism Compared to Racism and Sexism," *Journal of Gerontology,* V. 28(3), July, 1973, pp. 363–69.

This study also suggests that changes in our experiences of aging will come partly by attacking "institutional discrimination" against older people. Personnel practices that declare a man over forty "too old" to start a new job, retirement policies that do not transfer benefits from one job to the next or give benefits to surviving spouses, and schools that refuse admission to graduate-degree programs to women over thirty all contribute to the lower economic status of older persons.

Our behavior and the options open to us are thus influenced by the norms of our society. Other cultures have different norms and expectations. How does our society differ from others? Is the status of the aged the same in all societies? Is there some magic land where we may grow old in comfort and honor?

ACROSS CULTURES: WOULD YOU RATHER BE IN BALI?

Of course, if any of *us* were to move to Bali as older adults, our experiences as old persons would be different from those of a native, because we would not necessarily share the whole complex set of beliefs of the Bali culture. We might not know the folklore and magic rituals which the elderly must know in order to be honored. The problems of finding the ideal setting for growing older are very complex.

Donald Cowgill has developed an interesting theory of aging based upon research in many different cultures. He is interested in finding a set of generalizations about aging that would apply to all people throughout the world. On the basis of research so far, he has found some "universals" of aging, and other cultural "variables" which affect the status of the aged. Cowgill's major thesis is that the "role and status of the aged varies systematically with the degree of modernization of society." He found that modernization tends to decrease the relative status of the aged. Since we live in one of the most modernized societies in the history of the world, we may wish to think about what this can mean for our aging.

The following selection is a brief summary of the theory; the entire volume is of great interest.

A Theory of Aging in Cross-Cultural Perspective

Donald Cowgill

UNIVERSALS

It is difficult to discover any human behaviors which are truly universal; this is equally true of behavior of old people and behavior toward them.

Simmons maintains that there are recurrent basic interests which manifest themselves in old people in all societies: (1) to preserve life as long as possible, (2) to seek release from wearisome exertion and get protection from physical hazards, (3) to maintain active participation in group affairs, (4) to safeguard prerogatives—possessions, rights, prestige, and authority—and (5) to meet death honorably and comfortably.[3] However, these are generalized motives which he infers from observed behaviors; they do not describe actual behavior. Indeed, the behavior which supposedly results from these interests admittedly varies widely: "the basic interests of aging persons appear to be more uniform than are the solutions. . . ." Unfortunately, it is impossible to ascertain whether these so-called interests are real universal aspects of the phenomena of aging or are merely mental constructs of a single observer from a single cultural background.

As a prelude to generalizations concerning social behavior relating to old age, we may note that there are some demographic principles which appear to apply to all societies and which influence the social setting within which aging takes place. . . .

From: *Aging and Modernization* edited by Donald O. Cowgill and Lowell D. Holmes. © 1972 by Meredith Corporation. Reprinted by permission of Appleton-Century-Crofts, Educational Division, Meredith Corporation.

[3] Leo W. Simmons, "Aging in Modern Society" in *Toward Better Understanding of the Aging.* Seminar on the Aging, Aspen, Colorado, September 8–13, 1958. New York: Council on Social Work Education, 1959, p. 4.

UNIVERSALS:

1. The aged always constitute a minority within the total population.
2. In an older population, females outnumber males.
3. Widows comprise a high proportion of an older population.
4. In all societies, some people are classified as old and are treated differently because they are so classified.
5. There is a widespread tendency for people defined as old to shift to more sedentary, advisory, or supervisory roles involving less physical exertion and more concerned with group maintenance than with economic production.
6. In all societies, some old persons continue to act as political, judicial, and civic leaders.
7. In all societies, the mores prescribe some mutual responsibility between old people and their adult children.
8. All societies value life and seek to prolong it, even in old age.

SYSTEMATIC VARIATIONS

It is much easier to detect variation in ideas and behaviors concerning aging than to find uniformities. However, little is gained in terms of scientific theory by merely listing these variations at random; to be meaningful in terms of theory they must be placed in some coherent order or system. Simmons sought to do this for his 71 primitive societies by correlating aspects of aging with various characteristics of the physical, social, and cultural environment. However, these emerge as a kind of miscellany of correlations. The chief value is not in the principles derived from these correlations, but rather in delineating and illustrating the range of variation in primitive societies in attitudes toward and treatment of the aged. Even such generalizations as can be derived from correlations with climate, form of primitive economy, and kinship systems, cannot be extended to apply to more complex, modern societies. But general theory must apply to all societies, not just a limited kind of societies. We now have some limited theories and generalizations based on two widely divergent samples: (1) from primitive or non-industrial societies, and (2) from highly industrialized, urbanized, mostly western societies. It would appear that a useful approach toward more general theory might derive from the comparison of these two extremes. A description of the differences amounts to a generalization that such variations are correlated with the degree of modernization. If such generalizations accurately describe relationships between degrees of modernization (presumably closely related to national development) and conditions of aging, the propositions should not only describe differences between societies at different stages of modernization, but also should have predictive value for societies now in the process of modernization.

VARIATIONS:

1. The concept of old age is relative to the degree of modernization; a person is classified as old at an earlier chronological age in a primitive society than in a modern society.

2. Old age is identified in terms of chronological age chiefly in modern societies; in other societies onset of old age is more commonly linked with events such as succession to eldership or becoming a grandparent.

3. Longevity is directly and significantly related to the degree of modernization.

4. Modernized societies have older populations, i.e., higher proportions of old people.

5. Modern societies have higher proportions of women and especially of widows.

6. Modern societies have higher proportions of people who live to be grandparents and even great grandparents.

7. The status of the aged is high in primitive societies and is lower and more ambiguous in modern societies.

8. In primitive societies, older people tend to hold positions of political and economic power, but in modern societies such power is possessed by only a few.

9. The status of the aged is high in societies in which there is a high reverence for or worship of ancestors.

10. The status of the aged is highest when they constitute a low proportion of the population and tends to decline as their numbers and proportions increase.

11. The status of the aged is inversely proportional to the rate of social change.

12. Stability of residence favors high status of the aged; mobility tends to undermine it.

13. The status of the aged tends to be high in agricultural societies and lower in urbanized societies.

14. The status of the aged tends to be high in preliterate societies and to decline with increasing literacy of the populations.

15. The status of the aged is high in those societies in which they are able to continue to perform useful and valued functions; however, this is contingent upon the values of the society as well as upon the specific activities of the aged.

16. Retirement is a modern invention; it is found chiefly in modern high-productivity societies.

17. The status of the aged is high in societies in which the extended form of the family is prevalent and tends to be lower in societies which favor the nuclear form of the family and neolocal marriage.

18. With modernization the responsibility for the provision of economic security for dependent aged tends to be shifted from the family to the state.

19. The proportion of the aged who are able to maintain leadership roles declines with modernization.

20. In primitive societies the roles of widows tend to be clearly ascribed, but such role ascription declines with modernization; the widow's role in modern societies tends to be flexible and ambiguous.

21. The individualistic value system of western society tends to reduce the security and status of older people.

22. Disengagement is not characteristic of the aged in primitive or agrarian societies, but an increasing tendency toward disengagement appears to accompany modernization.

There are basic human needs of older people that need to be met, regardless of culture. These include the desire to maintain some involvement in the society; to serve some worthy purpose and to be valued; to preserve dignity and possessions; and to meet death honorably.

There are several aspects of Cowgill's points that are particularly provocative in terms of our modern American society. Cowgill reports that the status of the aged is lower with modernization, increased numbers and proportion of the elderly, and rapid social change. All these characterize our society, and there is every indication that they will become even more characteristic of our society in the future. Since we will not revert to a primitive society where few survive to old age, how can we improve the status of the elderly in a modern society? Do we have any reason to expect things to change? What should be done to make aging in our modernized society more pleasant for all?

If we examine Cowgill's list of "variations," we can find clues for raising the status of the elderly in our society. For example, since residential stability favors high status of the aged, we can encourage urban communities which include housing for all needs. Rather than segregating young adults in the city, growing families in the suburbs, and elders in "leisure villages," we can have all ages living together in the same community. By providing industry and business nearby, it would be possible for a family to live out its life cycle in the same community.

Residential proximity might do more to favor the extended family relationships; in such an arrangement, several generations live near enough to give mutual aid. Within such systems, older people tend to have higher status. If grandparents live nearby, they can be of assistance in child-rearing, providing a sense of continuity between past, present, and future for all involved. An alternative to extended-family relationships formed by genetic or "blood" ties is to encourage kinship-by-choice arrangements. Some communal organizations include several generations and have relationships resembling those of an extended family in more primitive societies.

The status of the elderly tends to be low in societies which emphasize an individualistic value system—the individual works for his own gratification and achievements, and failure of any kind is considered evidence of personal flaws. In such a value system, poverty, low occupational achievement, and mental illness can all be taken as evidence of personal inferiority and lack of diligence. Those who succeed "deserve" success, and those who are nonproductive deserve their poverty and can be ignored by the more "able." Social policies under such a system stress individual responsibility for coping with old age, rather than providing an equitable standard of living for all members of the society and looking for ways in which improved social structures can make aging less difficult.

Some societies stress sublimating individual achievement and working for the common good; the elderly, as well as the young and disabled, are provided for. As Cowgill points out:

> Individual life is viewed as a phase of an ongoing life process, the individual is of less intrinsic value, and his chief value is as a link between the past and the future. . . .[4] For example . . . in Russia individualism is suppressed in favor of the collective effort, and here we have a quite modern society which . . . also provides a security and satisfying status for its elders. It is significant to note that this status is maintained even though there is probably as strong an emphasis on the importance of work and the work role as in the West. . . .[5]

The individualistic value system is shifting somewhat in our society, to emphasize more our responsibility for one another. Recent efforts to extend Medicare and major medical insurance to all, to provide financial support for higher education, and to establish a minimum family income are evidence of this shift.

An alternate value system would stress the intrinsic worth of every human being, regardless of age, sex, color, weight, etc. Such a value system might be termed *humanistic,* and it would stress the provision of basic needs to every individual while maintaining individual freedoms of choice. Humanism as a social philosophy may be possible only in an affluent society such as ours. The elderly in a society with a humanistic value system should share equally in the resources and status of the society.

The status of the aged is higher when they continue to perform socially useful and valued functions. There are several alternatives open to the elderly in our society. They could be allowed to function within more traditional work roles by increasing the flexibility in work schedules, retirement policies, etc. They can perform many needed functions in the society which are not currently being met, such as acting as foster grandparents, "visitors" to shut-ins, and tutors for schoolchildren. Some areas have programs where older people are used as special teachers and consultants to schools and social agencies.

The status of the elderly tends to be high in preliterate societies partly because, in the absence of written language or books, the elders best know the tribal heritage. They are the ones charged with passing on the religious ritual, history, survival skills, and artistic forms. There

---

[4] Donald Cowgill and Lowell Holmes, *Aging and Modernization,* p. 12.
[5] *Ibid.,* p. 320.

are, even in our highly literate society, many skills which can only be passed on from generation to generation by personal instruction. Currently a part of our American heritage is being lost because the older craftsmen are not teaching younger people their skills. We need centers where people skilled in handwork and crafts could teach younger people this aspect of our heritage.

The older adults in our society may be gaining status because they are *not* working. As work becomes devalued and leisure becomes more important, the segment of the population which is retired may become the new "leisure class."

3

biological changes: the spirit is willing but the flesh is weak

The cartoon of an obviously middle-aged woman gazing into the glass and saying, "Mirror, mirror on the wall, lie to me," speaks poignantly to the physical changes we experience with age. The negative stereotypes of aging always include biological decline, when our body no longer responds quickly to our wishes and our altered appearance announces that we are no longer young. We will consider here what changes are typical in body appearance and functioning generally. We will also look more closely at changes in intellectual functioning and effects of changed production of reproductive hormones.

Many have commented—or charged—that we live in a youth-oriented culture which prizes and rewards physical vigor and youthful beauty. Mass advertising sells us products designed to defer the signs of aging. The message is clear: to grow old gracefully is not to grow old. Many, like the cartoon heroine, may wish to deny the signs of aging.

Biological changes are important. Most obviously, changes in energy level, ability of the body to recover from stress, and less effective sensory systems affect the ease with which we cope with daily problems. Biological changes associated with normal aging seldom mean we *cannot* deal with life, but it may require more thought and more effort to accomplish at sixty what we did without strain at thirty. (Like the seventy-two-year-old man who commented that "Now it takes my

wife and me all night to do what we used to do all night.") Many individuals learn to adapt to biological changes by conserving their energies and using themselves efficiently; also, many watch their health
and physical functioning more closely as they get older.

Physical changes, perhaps more importantly, affect the image we
hold of ourself. A child will be very concerned if he breaks a leg or
undergoes surgery, fearing that because a part of him is "not good,"
perhaps he, as a whole, is "not good" either. The feelings we form
about ourselves are tied to our experiences with our body. This experiencing of our body includes the sensual pleasures we receive (the satisfied feelings of a good meal well digested, or the excitement-relaxation
cycle of sexuality); it also includes the discomfort of constipation or
shortness of breath. It includes the messages we receive from other people, who compliment us on our shape or glossy hair, or who avoid gazing on our shrunken, crippled arm.

As adults, we remain concerned about our bodies. If we experience our bodies as "good," as acceptable and pleasurable, this helps us
feel good about ourselves as a whole. Some people rely a great deal on
their body concept for their self-image (e.g. athletes); others, such as
artists or scholars, give much less importance to body functioning and
more to intellectual or emotional aspects in forming their self-image.
Most people probably regard their bodies as important, but not as the
most important part of themselves.

WHO IS AVERAGE?

Anne is sixty-nine. She is in a hospital, recovering from a cerebral
thrombosis and pneumonia. After her first thrombosis, she couldn't
walk; now, she has difficulty talking. She has suffered from arteriosclerosis for the past five years; memory loss coupled with visual loss
sometimes leads her to report what seem like hallucinations.

Mark is seventy-four. He is in a nursing home, fighting and losing a battle with cancer. Although he is mobile, the carcinoma on his
throat does not allow him to swallow liquids; he must be fed by a
direct tube to his stomach. He is lucid and enjoys conversation and
watching the ball games on TV. As the cancer progresses, however, he
will be increasingly sedated and will find it hard to recognize his family. He will refuse the final operation that is offered him.

Simon is eighty-five. He still spends several days a week at his company offices, and golfs whenever he gets the chance. Although he is slower and not as strong as he once was, he can accomplish what he wishes. Except for slight rheumatism, he finds few problems with his body.

Susan is nintey-five. This year, for the first time, she has decided not to do canning as usual. She lives alone, in a house that adjoins her daughter's, and does her housework herself. One day she walks to her daughter's house and dies in a chair, so quietly that the daughter thinks she is merely dozing.

Which of these people is an average old person? We can talk about the average six-year-old fairly easily, but talking about the average seventy-year-old is often absurd. Right now, it is fairly hard to distinguish the results of age from the results of disease; a major difference between Anne, Simon, Mark, and Susan is the degree of disease that they suffer from. Although there are several kinds of physiological processes that generally decline with age, individual characteristics may make the decline slow or fast. To separate individual aging from general aging effects, much longitudinal research is needed. Several large-scale studies have been carried out; usually they focus on people at various ages and follow them for several years. Since these people are volunteers, some drop out as they get bored, or ill, or if they move away or die. It is likely that these volunteers are healthier than the general population and that those who stay with a research program are healthier than the ones who drop out. Other research looks at nursing homes and hospitals; these subjects are also not representative. Still another kind of research looks at small communities where there seems to be marked longevity; the Georgian highlands of the Caucasus mountains is a well-known example. Finally, evidence about age changes comes from animal research, in which the experimenter can observe many generations in a short period of time and can manipulate the environment or induce certain diseases.

More people are living longer today, but few people live past 100. Although the average life span has increased rapidly in the twentieth century, most of the increase so far is due to advances in pediatric medicine, nutrition, and the development of drugs which combat the killers of childhood and young adulthood. Comparatively little has been discovered about the problems of advancing age.

BIOLOGICAL THEORIES OF AGING

There are several theories to account for the physical changes that come with age; none of these theories is wholly adequate but each contributes to our understanding of aging. Some theories stress hereditary factors, pointing to genetic differences in resistances to disease and longevity of individual cells. Other theories emphasize the accumulation of waste materials in the body cells, which eventually clogs the cells and causes them to die from lack of nutrients; researchers are trying to find ways to purify the body cells and thus retard (or reverse?) physical aging. Some theories stress disease resistance, and see aging as primarily a problem of coping with diseases. Presumably we could prolong life if the antibodies could be strengthened and the disease processes stopped.

THE EFFECTS OF AGING

As we age, phyiscal changes are almost inevitable. Physical capacity in many areas is at its peak in adolescence; hearing acuity is said to be strongest at age ten.

Many of the changes result in decreasing homeostatic capacities. Homeostasis describes the balanced state of the body as it returns to normal after a period of stress or exertion. It is comparable to the thermostat in a home: when the air becomes cold, the thermostat turns on the furnace to make the air comfortably warm again. As the air becomes warm, the thermostat turns off the furnace so that it will not overheat. Many of the body systems operate to keep the right "balance" in the body.

As we age, it takes more effort for the body to return to normal. Thus, stress, exertion, and change are experienced as more intense. More old people die in heat waves because their bodies do not adjust to temperature extremes.

As you may have already noticed, the body burns up food less efficiently as you grow older. No longer can you consume the quantities of food of early adolescence. If you eat the same amount of food and maintain the same level of activity, you will gain weight by middle age. This is simply because the body does not need the same caloric intake, and the excess turns to fat. You will have to reduce your food intake still further in old age if you do not wish to gain weight.

Wrinkled skin is a visible "cue" of aging. As we age, the skin cells become thinner. Wrinkles are caused by the loss of below-the-skin fat and the inability of the skin to "snap back." Because individual cells gradually lose the ability to multiply, wounds heal more slowly, and scar tissue formed is weaker.

Another common symptom of aging is slowed response. For example, an older person crossing the street may find it difficult to get all the way across in the time allotted for one green light. By the time the information has "registered" that the light has changed, part of the time (for crossing) has elapsed. The slower movements of the elderly add to the problem. They may instead cross in two lights. These difficulties are not the result of indifference or laziness, but reflect changes in nerve cells.

Unlike most body cells, nerve cells do not reproduce themselves; when they die or are destroyed they will not be replaced. By age seventy, some 20 percent of the neurons present at birth have died; since the neurons conduct sensory impulses and "information" to muscles, the brain, and other tissues, it is likely that the loss of neurons shows in behavior. The neurons are replaced by cells which do not conduct nerve impulses, but merely occupy space. Thus, slowed reaction time is predictable in old age. You can still get where you're going, and remember what you went for—but it will take you longer.

"Oh, my creaking joints!" is an exclamation of the old rather than the young. Indeed, the soft cartilage tissue that connects the bones at the joints (like the "gristle" at the end of the chicken leg) becomes thinner and less flexible. This may lead to pain when the joints are moved. Though it may hurt to move such joints, inactivity results in further degeneration and more pain. The ribs are more likely to break, since the cartilage is unable to absorb extra pressure.

Bones may become more porous and brittle, as calcium is withdrawn. This is a problem for women after the menopause especially; something about estrogens help bones remain healthy. Bones break more easily and heal more slowly.

Hearts may or may not break with age; many become weakened. The heart muscles are partly replaced by fat, and the heart has trouble providing proper amounts of oxygenated blood. Thus, the hands and feet are likely to feel cold, breathlessness is more common, and the heart itself receives a lowered oxygen supply. The arteries and veins may become clogged, especially with fatty cells; this condition is thought to be related to fat intake in earlier years. Heart attacks are related to clogged blood vessels. Several studies indicate that the risk of heart disease can be lowered by not smoking, exercising moderately and consistently, and following a moderate-calorie, low-fat diet. The earlier in life these rules are followed, the less is the risk of heart trouble later.

Food may not taste the same as one ages. It's not necessarily that the food is different, but the aging lose some taste buds. Ordinarily, there are about 250 tastebuds in each papilla (on the tongue), but by old age the number may drop to 100. The cells in the digestive system (stomach, intestines, bowels) are constantly being replaced. However, the digestive system is very sensitive to emotional states, and the person who is lonely, depressed, or worried may experience an upset stomach. Digestion is also affected by nutrition—at all ages. A diet of coffee and pastry is completely inadequate for older people; older people who live alone sometimes find it difficult to shop and cook meals for one, and so resort to a diet of "snacking" foods which is bad for health.

Sensory systems are less acute with advancing age. The sense of smell may become less good; this affects the sense of taste. (Try eating with your nose held closed.) The eyes change, and one of the first signs of advancing age is realizing one can't quite see the world. As Ogden Nash puts it so wittily:[1]

> Middle-aged life is merry, and I love to lead it,
> But there comes a day when your eyes are all right but your arm isn't
> long enough to hold the telephone book where you can read it . . .

EFFECTS OF CHANGE

Because stress becomes harder to cope with as we grow older; because change is a major contributor to stress; and because various fundamental changes (e.g., deaths of friends or spouse) become increasingly likely with age—it is important that we look at the overall effects of change on such things as coping with stress and the onset of disease.

Young people are aware that they may seek change as a relief from boredom or pain, as a challenge, or as a mildly pleasurable pur-

[1] Ogden Nash, "Peekaboo, I Almost See You," *The Private Dining Room and Other New Verses* (Curtis Publishing Co., 1949).

suit. Changes may involve initial discomfort but the result may be well worth it. Older people may also seek change for similar reasons. Both young and old may resist changes which make them feel very uncomfortable, challenge their ability to cope, and make them feel inadequate. No one wants to feel inadequate.

Change can be experienced as stressful. Some people seem to tolerate changes with little evidence of stress, and others need a very stable situation in order to remain free of stress. Stress can make people sick, physically and emotionally.

> The death rate of widows and widowers is 10 times higher during the first year of bereavement than for others their age; divorced persons have an illness rate 12 times higher than married persons in the year following divorce, and up to 80% of serious physical illnesses seem to develop at a time when victims feel helpless and hopeless.
>
> Dr. Thomas Holmes, a psychiatrist, and his colleagues have devised a system to help predict illnesses related to stress. The Social Readjustment Rating Scale lists 43 life events associated with disruption in the average person's life. The scale was constructed by having hundreds of persons of different ages, cultures, and walks of life rank the relative amount of adjustment necessitated by various life events.
>
> In studies dating back to the 1940's, Dr. Holmes has found, as have other researchers in the field, that a clustering of life events often precedes the onset of diseases, ranging from heart attacks to illness and infections as well as psychiatric disturbances. . . . His studies indicate that an accumulation of 200 or more life change units in a single year may be more disruption than a single individual can withstand. . . . Dr. Holmes's theory is that change—no matter whether it is for good or for bad—is stressful to the biological organism and makes it more susceptible to the onslaught of disease.[2]

We can use Holmes's "Stress Scale" below to estimate the likely amount of stress in different stages of life, though we cannot account for individual differences in stress tolerance. At age fifty, *you* may react to a divorce, remarriage and honeymoon, new job, new apartment, grandparenthood, and vegetarianism taking place in one year (total score of 258, including Christmas) with zest and renewed interest in life; your *cousin* might collapse with an attack of colitis.

[2] Edited from Jane Brody, "Doctors Study Treatment of Ills Brought on by Stress," *The New York Times*, June 10, 1973, p. 20.

THE STRESS OF ADJUSTING TO CHANGE

Events	Scale of Impact
Death of spouse	100
Divorce	73
Marital separation	65
Jail term	63
Death of close family member	63
Personal injury or illness	53
Marriage	50
Fired at work	47
Marital reconciliation	45
Retirement	45
Change in health of family member	44
Pregnancy	40
Sex difficulties	39
Gain of new family member	39
Business readjustment	39
Change in financial state	38
Death of close friend	37
Change to different line of work	36
Change in number or arguments with spouse	35
Mortgage over $10,000	31
Foreclosure of mortgage or loan	30
Change in responsibilities at work	29
Son or daughter leaving home	29
Trouble with in-laws	29
Outstanding personal achievement	28
Wife begins or stops work	26
Begin or end school	26
Change in living conditions	25
Revision of personal habits	24
Trouble with boss	23
Change in work hours or conditions	20
Change in residence	20
Change in schools	20
Change in recreation	19
Change in church activities	19
Change in social activities	18
Mortgage or loan less than $10,000	17
Change in sleeping habits	16
Change in number of family get-togethers	15
Change in eating habits	15
Vacation	13
Christmas	12
Minor violations of the law	11

Source: Scale reprinted from T. H. Holmes and R. H. Rahe, "The Social Readjustment Rating Scale," *Journal of Psychosomatic Research*, 11: 1967, 213–18. Used by permission of Dr. Holmes.

REPRODUCTIVE AND SEXUAL SYSTEMS

Biological changes can affect your adult sex life for the worse—but usually only if you let them. As will be evident from the next chapter, human sexuality is not closely tied to biology, and most of us can expect to maintain good sexual functioning into our old age. There are few medical conditions which cause sexual activity to be eliminated; a person may need to modify his sexual style, but he can expect to continue sexual pleasures.

The Prostate Problem. The most likely problem for men is the enlargement of the prostate gland. The prostate surrounds the urethra (urinary outlet) in the abdominal cavity; within it lie the ejaculatory ducts. At the time of ejaculation, fluids are released from the prostate, the seminal vesicles, the epididymis, and other male genital glands. Enlargement of this gland is very common, beginning in middle age, and may interfere with the free flow of urine. The gland may become cancerous. The traditional method of treatment has been removal of all or part of the prostate by surgery. This is a very threatening procedure for most men because the incisions are made near the genital area. Few men really understand the functioning of the prostate gland, or the consequences of the surgery.

Unfortunately, few doctors discuss the sexual consequences of medical procedures with patients, and many patients are too embarrassed to ask. Some doctors have told men they will become impotent after this operation; this can be a self-fulfilling prophecy, since fear of failure is the surest way to fail. After prostate surgery many men are still able to obtain erections, to have orgasms, and to ejaculate.

Surgical procedures vary, and some have more drastic consequences than others. If you face prostate surgery, inquire carefully about the procedures and the likely consequences. Shop around for a doctor who will explain things to you and who is concerned for your continuing sexual functioning. Don't believe that "you're too old to care anyway."

Wives should be sympathetic and understanding about prostate problems. While any malfunctioning of the body, and surgical procedures necessitated by this, are frightening, when these involve the genital areas the threat can be profound. Wives can do a great deal to avoid secondary impotence in their husbands (psychologically induced) by responding to them as sexual persons and expecting them to remain sexy.

If erection abilities are impaired, there are forms of stimulation (oral and manual) which can result in orgasm and mutual sexual pleasure. Total body massage can provide great sensual pleasure for both partners, and can continue throughout life regardless of impotence or various medical disabilities.

The Menopause. In women the reproductive system ceases to function around the age of forty-five to fifty-five. The gradual cessation of the menstrual periods is called the *menopause.* The term "climacterium" refers more generally to the variety of changes which occur during this time.

The ovaries begin to atrophy (wither), they cease producing ova, and the amount of estrogen produced is greatly reduced. The reduction in estrogen can result in sagging breasts, more facial hair, lowered voice level, and tender vaginal tissues. However, judicious hormone-replacement therapy or application of estrogen creams to the vagina often resolves these changes.

The erratic and unpredictable production of hormones during this period cause the infamous "hot flashes and cold sweats." They are not in the mind, but are physical. Most women appreciate understanding husbands during these times, and most women soon recover to feel in better health than they had known for many years.

Perhaps the last statement seems surprising—particularly to those who are not familiar with any women who have gone through the menopause and told them about it. Like many other aspects of aging, the menopause may seem worse to the young than to those actually experiencing it.

What difference does menopause make? To find out, we can review some research on natural menopause. Also, we can look at women who have undergone premature, surgical menopause with hysterectomy (removal of the uterus).

There are still many "old wives' tales" about the menopause that turn out not to be true of most old wives. For example, much of the psychiatric literature describes the menopause as a terrible trauma for a woman because she can no longer bear children. Presumably her husband will no longer see her as sexy, and her days of Womanhood are over when the menstrual cycle stops.

This turns out to be nonsense, of course. Systematic research on women in various stages of the menopause was carried out at the University of Chicago.[3] Overall, the researchers concluded that women attach little significance to the menopause. Other events in the lives of these women produced emotional stress, but seldom the lack of reproductive ability.

Many of the women found the physical symptoms annoying, but were relieved to have the menstrual nuisance end. Many felt a renewed interest in sexuality; this is often related to freedom from fear of pregnancy, greater privacy after the children have left), and accepting their bodies.

If natural menopause does not seem to meet the psychiatric stereotypes, what about artificial menopause? Perhaps women can adjust to removal of their reproductive organs only because they are getting older anyway. Total hysterectomy involves the surgical removal of the ovaries and uterus, thus removing reproductive capability and hormone production suddenly. It is a procedure which is not uncommon in women over thirty, and is usually performed because of suspected malignant growth. Hormone replacement therapy is typical to retard the signs of aging in skin texture, muscle tone, and secondary sex characteristics.

Gynecological and nursing texts generally advise future medical caretakers that the woman who undergoes a hysterectomy will suffer a severe blow to her sense of femininity and wholeness, and should be treated with tender regard and pity. Two of my students, Caryn Eschen and Rena Tabachnik explored the impact of surgical menopause on a woman's feelings about herself by interviewing women who had undergone hysterectomies.[4] Hysterectomies were viewed much more negatively than natural menopause, but it seemed clear that the threat centered more on operative procedures and the fear of cancer than on the loss of reproductive abilities. Only one of the ten women felt that after the hysterectomy a woman is not a "real woman" anymore.

These women experienced a great deal of discomfort with their menstrual periods before the operation and during the recovery period; in particular, they commonly experienced mood swings, physical symptoms, and anxiety until the proper dose of replacement estrogen was

[3] Bernice Neugarten, V. Wood, R. Kraines, & B. Loomis, "Women's Attitudes Toward the Menopause," *Vita Humana*, 6 (1963), pp. 140–51.

[4] Margaret Hellie Huyck, Caryn Eschen, and Rena Tabachnik, "Women's Attitudes Toward Radical Hysterectomy," presented at the 26th Annual Scientific Meetings of the Gerontological Society, Miami, Florida, Nov. 7, 1973.

finally established through trial and error. They appreciated the support and help given by their husbands during this period, but many felt guilty about their own (temporary) inability to continue caring for their home and family. After the postoperative recovery period, however, most of the women agreed that they felt better than they had for years, that life was more interesting and more enjoyable; the interviews made it clear that these women felt they had faced possible death and had a renewed appreciation of life and their own improved health.

Thus, for most women who experienced artificial and natural menopause, the anticipation was worse than the reality, and recovery resulted in rewarding consequences. However, some women reacted very negatively to menopause and to hysterectomy. Such women may be the ones who end up in the doctor's office with their problems, and thus probably color the clinical impressions of menopause.

One of the ten women in this study fit perfectly into the stereotype of the hysterectomy "victim." She viewed the hysterectomy as a direct threat to her self-esteem, having tied her worth to her reproductive ability. Her sexual activity, unlike that of the other women, decreased after her recuperative period; she explained that she could no longer feel the way she used to, now that she was "empty." She felt that she had greatly aged, that her physical attractiveness and diminished and her energy level had declined. She attributed all these changes to the hysterectomy. She had had a partial hysterectomy the year before in hopes of not needing a complete one, even though her doctor had warned her that a complete hysterectomy would be necessary. She said that she had never discussed her operation with anyone except her doctor and her husband, and her tone implied guilt and shame over the operation.

Why these different reactions? Age, employment, activities, or number of children do not seem to account for them. Further research should explore the experience of menopause for childless women, whether childless by choice or accident; the mothers in these studies, for example, assumed that natural or surgical menopause would be worse for women who had not borne children.

Stern and Prados[5] suggest that it is not the menopause that causes difficulties in middle age, but the women's personality. One psychiatrist reported that 95 percent of the women who were psychoneurotic at the time of the menopause had psychoneurotic symptoms before en-

---

[5] K. Stern and M. Prados, "Personality Studies in Menopausal Women," *American Journal of Psychiatry,* 103, 1946, pp. 358–68.

tering the menopausal phase; whereas none of the women who were not psychoneurotic at the time of the menopause had had earlier psychoneurotic symptoms. Kraines[6] concluded that the different reactions to the menopause suggest different life-styles for coping with physical and emotional problems, since she found significant relationships between reaction to menopause and previous health problems, difficulty with menstruation, and reactions during pregnancy.

There seems to be consistency of coping styles within the individual, so that past reactions are predictive of attitudes, reactions, and self-evaluations when faced with an issue such as hysterectomy or the climacterium. Hormonal changes and surgical procedures do present predictable problems for every individual, but they do not become a crisis for most. The coping style you are now developing is the best predictor of how you will handle the menopause—your own or your lover's.

Male Menopause. What about men? Clearly men do not have a "menopause," since they have no menstrual cycle to cease. However, here is considerable lively debate as to hormone changes in middle age which may "conspire" with cultural factors to make it a time of upset for men—and for their wives and employers. Martha Weinman Lear reviews, delightfully, the controversy and the evidence.

Is There a Male Menopause? Or, what is going on when the glands, the genes, the mind and the culture conspire?

Martha Weinman Lear

My friends had been married for 19 years; a good marriage as marriages go, or so she thought and so their circle believed. Mutual interests, a satisfactory sex life, flowers every Valentine's Day, two nice children, two successful careers, a country house, a retirement plan.

[6] Ruth Kraines, "The Menopause and Evaluation of the Self: A Study of Women in the Climacteric Years," 1963, Unpublished Doctoral Dissertation, University of Chicago, Committee on Human Development.

. . . Then one day he announced that he wanted to split, and split. More to her agony, he went off with a woman young enough, she says, to be their daughter. She is sure she knows the reason: It's the menopause.

We say it rather as we say, "It's the bug," or, "It's the heat," or, "It's those men in Washington," disposing of unhappy phenomena with minimal fuss. Now, the medical profession does not agree, and never has agreed, as to whether anything that may properly be called a male menopause actually exists, but certainly the idea has wide currency. A man of a certain age becomes depressed: It's menopause. He loses his sex drive: It's menopause. He regains it with a woman half his age. Indeed, it's menopause.

Every recent study shows that divorces, extramarital affairs, male personality disturbances (most notably, depression), male sex problems peak most sharply between ages 40 to 60, and in the popular literature such statistics often are tied in an ambiguous way to something called a "male crisis" or "male menopausal syndrome." Even the recent H.E.W. report on work malaise, "Work in America," hints at something of the sort, although without defining it: "A general feeling of obsolescence appears to overtake middle managers when they reach their late 30's. Their careers appear to have reached a plateau, and they realize that life from here on will be a long and inevitable decline. There is a marked increase in the death rate between the ages of 35 to 40 for employed men, apparently as a result of this 'midlife crisis'. . . ."

Male menopause: Does it exist? The term itself is patently absurd: What has never been cannot cease to be. "Menopause syndrome" really is not fortuitous either—not for either sex, implying as it does that menopause causes the syndrome. The arrest of menses is not a cause, after all, but a symptom—merely the most visible evidence of hormonal change. In the medical journals of a number of European countries, they call it "climacterium virile." (Not that they *necessarily* understand it any better than we; an article in a German medical journal was entitled *"Zur Frage des 'Climacterium Verile.'"* Climacterium, according to Webster: the bodily and psychic involutional changes accompanying the transition from middle age to old age.) Certainly the term, "male climactic syndrome," seems less an assault on biology than anything involving the word "menopause."

At any rate, a definition: The male climacteric syndrome is a cluster of physiologic, constitutional and psychological symptoms occurring in some men aged approximately 45 to 60, associated with hormonal changes and often closely resembling the female climacteric syndrome.

The symptoms: nervousness, decrease or loss of sexual potential, depressions, decreased memory and concentration, decreased or absent libido, fatigue, sleep disturbances, irritability, loss of interest and self-confidence, indecisiveness, numbness and tingling, fear of impending danger, excitability; less often, headaches, vertigo, tachycadia, constipation, crying, hot flashes, chilly sensations, itching, sweating, cold hands and feet. . . .

In the beginning, there was a clear-cut etiology. In the late nineteen-thirties, internist August A. Werner of the St. Louis University School of Medicine described the male climacteric syndrome as a clinical entity caused by endocrine imbalance, the chief factor in this imbalance being insufficient production of male sex hormones. Citing all of the above symptoms and more, Dr. Werner wrote: "With the exception of [cessation of] menstruation in the female, it is the same for the two sexes."

Later the literature (it is scant) began stressing the interplay of physiological and psychological factors. In a 1947 study based on 30 cases of men with climacteric symptoms, two Canadian psychiatrists reported that hormonal therapy relieved the general symptoms in every case, but did little to relieve the psychological symptoms: "The history of these [psychologically disturbed] patients frequently showed a compulsive trend for achievement and success. They were ambitious, active, aggressive, hard workers, good family providers. . . . Close examination of these patients showed that the glandular disturbance had mobilized and brought to the surface old longings and anxieties that were only partly overcome, or incompletely sublimated, during the previous years of apparent emotional equilibrium. . . ." In other words, perhaps the male climacteric, while triggered by hormonal changes, correlated in some way with personality factors, as in ulcers, or with socioeconomic factors, as in gout.

In more recent years, the questions have multiplied. Depression, for example, is perhaps the most pervasive emotional disturbance of the climacteric years: Is it a *special* depression, demonstrably part of a syndrome? Or is it what one skeptic calls "just your garden-variety, middle-aged depression"? Or do both say the same thing?

Geriatric psychiatrist Alvin Goldfarb of Mount Sinai Hospital in Manhattan, who has written extensively in the field, speaks of "that malaise, you know, that descends upon a man when he reaches that point at which he knows he either has a chance or no ghost of a chance to be President, he knows if he's fulfilled what the sociologists call his 'ascribed role,' and he may also—much to his distress—have a pretty good idea of how long he's going to live." Seen in this way, the climacteric depression is a given, one of the existential inevitabilities. But if that is what we are talking about, why does it strike some men and not others?

Again, the sexual symptons: Physiologically, given good health and an amenable partner, a man should be able to function sexually until he dies of old age. But the production of male sex hormones (testosterone) *is* diminishing gradually from roughly age 40 on; spermatogenesis is decreasing (at age 70, the sperm count is about one-third of what it was at 35), and there are the familiar changes in sexual response: It takes progressively longer to be aroused, longer to ejaculate, longer to revive sexual tension. Normal, all of these.

But add to them what urologist Harold Lear, director of the Human Sexuality Program at Mount Sinai's department of community medicine, calls the social overlays, and the changes are compounded. Dr. Lear refers to a study in which, asked to complete the sentence, "Sex for older people is . . . ," college students most commonly used the words "unimportant," "negligible" and "past."

"So many American men approaching middle age have been programmed to believe that their sex lives will become exactly that: unimportant, negligible and past," he says. "It becomes a self-fulfilling prophecy—the male may panic at the signs of decreased sexual power, and grow impotent; or he may act out vigorously and desperately in an attempt to reaffirm his threatened masculinity."

Thus, who is the climacteric male? The man whose sexual powers have diminished? Or the man who is impotent and miserable about it? Or the man who, at age 50, can't do and doesn't care? Further, what is the cause of the sex problems—the physiological factor, or the pscho-logical, or the cultural?

Most current thinking holds that the climacteric implicates (if it implicates anything) all of these factors. But as to *how* they are implicated, and why, and in what pattern of cause and effect, there is very little agreement and a great deal of professional bias.

These are the currently prevalent theories; they are not an attempt to box in the theoreticians, most of whom are—within limits—flexible.

THE HORMONAL FACTOR

In most menopausal women, the production of estrogen (female sex hormones) drops off abruptly—not overnight, by any means, but fast enough to provide compelling reason for many of their tensions and discomforts (75 percent of women are said to have an acute estrogen deficiency within a few years after the onset of menopause). But in the male, the decline of testosterone production is gradual and progressive. Rates of decline vary, but politely: no hormonal histrionics, no clear-cut cause for the sloughs of despair. This contrast between slow change and sudden change is absolutely central to the argument as to whether a male climacteric is a genuine clinical event. In essence, the hormonal theory holds that there is unquestionably a male climacteric; that it is caused exclusively by hormonal decline; and that, while hormonal change in the male is not so dramatic as in the female, it is dramatic enough to produce all the classic symptoms.

Herbert S. Kupperman, associate professor of medicine at New York University Medical Center, chief of endocrinology at three hospitals and consultants at a dozen others: "We see loss of sexual potenia; indeciveness—these men *hate* to make a decision; irritability; vasomotor symptoms in some; general ineptness . . . insecurity, uncertainty. There is no doubt in my mind—none—that these symptoms are due to the decline in testosterone production. As in women, the severity of the symptoms will depend on the rate of decline. Give hormonal replacement therapy, and the symptoms will improve. We get these results in blind tests, where he patients have no idea what they're getting.

"But: This is so only for the true climacteric. If you take a hundred impotent men and treat them with testosterone, 18 percent will respond. But if you do tests and treat only those with a hormonal deficiency, you will get a 90 percent repsonse. When a man is impotent with his wife but doing well with other women, that's no climacteric. When a man says that he can't get erections with women but wakes up with spontaneous erections—that man has no true climacteric. It's up here," pointing to his head.

To understand the "true" climacteric in Dr. Kupperman's terms, one must understand at least the fundamentals of male hormonal function. I use the assembly-line metaphor, which is primitive and overworked—Woody Allen recently used a space-ship variation to tell us everything we wanted to know about ejaculation—but handy nonetheless.

Hypothalmus: the boss of the endocrinological system. It controls the pituitary gland and operates, of course, under the ultimate jurisdiction of the brain.

Pituitary gland: the foreman. It stimulates most of the endocrine glands to function, and thus to produce hormones.

Endocrine glands: the workers. In response to instructions from the pituitary gland, various workers produce various hormones. Among them are the gonads or sex glands (testes in the male, ovaries in the female), which produce estrogen and testosterone.

Instructions: pituitary secretions which stimulate hormonal production. Those which stimulate sex-hormonal production are called pituitary gonadatropins.

So long as the chain of command is maintained and the gonads are healthy enough to follow instructions, sex hormones will be produced at the normal rate. The male climacteric syndrome occurs (*if it occurs*) when the testes, for whatever reason, stop normal production. For whatever reason: It is a weighty clause.

In the male of climacteric age, testosterone production may decline because (1) skewed instructions, or no instructions, are being sent to the testes; or because (2) the system is in an emergency, and testosterone production is inhibited while the pituitary concentrates on speeding up the production of some other hormone that is urgently needed—adrenal cortisone, for example, which defends the organism against stress; or because, (3) the testes themselves fail to obey instructions to function at the normal rate. "Produce," says the pituitary, sending plenty of gonadatropin down the line. "We can't," say the testes. "We're too old and tired." It is the third condition, and *only* the third (it is know as primary testicular insufficiency), which Kupperman defines as the "true" male climacteric.

The distinction is crucial. By dismissing the other two conditions (known as secondary testicular insufficiency), he virtually rules out any emotional cause for the male climacteric. Inhibition of normal sex-hormone production *could* be in response to some emotional imperative; as noted, stress is one possibility. But failure of the *testes* to perform is a totally physiological event. A man who is in acute or chronic stress, which may cause a testosterone deficiency, which may cause impaired sexual performance, which may cause depression, is not, by Kupperman's definition, a man in the climacteric: He is a depressed man.

It is as pure and self-contained a view of the male climacteric as currently exists. Certainly it satisfies the yearning for parameters. But many other physicians—psychiatrists, primarily—would consider it far too narrow. They feel that we need a definition at least broad enough to embrace the man who may be functioning adequately in his testicles, but wretchedly in his life.

THE PSYCHOLOGICAL FACTOR

This theory rests on the assumption that male endocrine changes simply are not precipitous enough to account for such symptoms as depression, nervousness and irritability. Hormonal decline will cause the loss of sexual and other energies, yes; but nothing more. Psychiatrist Helen Kaplan, director of the Paine-Whitney Sex-Therapy Clinic, Cornell Medical School, says: "If the definition is an abrupt, age-related change in the reproductive biology, then there is no male climacteric. If the definition is a psychophysiological constellation that occurs in our culture, in some men—then there is. The psychological symptoms are a reaction to the physiological symptoms.

"A man in these years has to give up so much control—control over his children, over his body, over his world. He may feel anger, and despair because he sees no solution. He builds defenses against these feelings, and one sees not a hopeless person but a man having affairs, racing around frantically, drinking too much. When the defenses break down, the anxiety shows through. But a well-integrated man adjusts to the decline in control and sexual power; he has no male climacteric."

A different equation, then: Aging plus neurosis equals the male climacteric. Kupperman yields somewhat. He says: "If a man has been inadequate from the start, he *may* be more likely to get a severe climacteric depression than well-adjusted men. But they can get it, too." No, they can't, say the psychiatrists.

(Many physicians make the same assumption about women. Mount Sinai psychiatrist Lawrence Roose: "Whenever you see a case of menopausal depression and take a careful history, you will invariably find that this isn't the first occurrence. These are the women who have had latent or open depressions at puberty, at marriage, at childbirth . . . at every critical point of their lives." Dr. Kaplan isn't sure. Severe depression doesn't come from the hormones, she agrees; but the rapid female endocrine change can at least "shake up" even a reasonably stable woman. Indeed, every normal woman spends roughly half her life experiencing a kind of "minimenopause" each month, when she is deprived of estrogen during menstruation; and the geometric rise in crimes, murders, suicides committed by women during the menses is well-documented. So why not at least a bit of agitation with the onset of maximenopause?)

"Some people think it's biologically ordained that everyone will become depressed in the middle years," says geriatric psychiatrist Goldfarb. "But the more I see, the more I think that some individuals just can't get clinically depressed. Others get depressed for no apparent reason. With still others, there may be reasons, but the trigger can be trivial because there is a cellular readiness for it: a genetic in-building, exactly analogous to the predisposition for diabetes. If a man inherits a manic-depressive pattern but has excellent nurture, the symptoms may never show. But if his nurture has not been so good, he is very likely to show symptons in his middle years, when we all begin to look backward and forward. He is more genetically vulnerable than other men to the stimuli which may depress us."

Dr. Goldfarb does not like the term "climacteric" (and many physicians agree with him), not because of the word itself but because any label conjures up too monolithic an image. "It's too mythical, somehow," he says. "It connotes a simple explanation for a scheme which is so exceedingly complex."

This brings everything back into definition. Psychiatric theory at least tells us why Smith will have disturbing personality changes in a serenely declining hormonal milieu, while Jones experiences hardly any change at all. At which point an endocrinologist might say: But Smith is neurotic, after all; these disturbing changes may have nothing to do with the true male climacteric. A psychiatrist might say: Well, of course Smith is neurotic; these disturbing changes *are* the true male climacteric. And yet another psychiatrist might say: Yes, Smith is neurotic, and these disturbing changes happen in just this way. But let's not give the thing a label.

THE SOCIOCULTURAL FACTOR

With the women's movement has come a re-examination of menopause
—as, indeed, of all sex-linked phenomena—within the feminist context. The nervous, ill-tempered, weepy woman who is summoned into
our imagination by the phrase, "She is menopausal," is seen not so
much as the victim of her hormones but as the victim of her social role.
The irritable, depressed, impotent (chronically or situationally) male
is seen in precisely the same terms.

No physician—at least, none whom I have interviewed—would
deny the hormones their due entirely. That is, they all agree that vasomotor symptoms—hot flashes and the like—are due to hormonal deficiency. But many of them insist that when we talk about *psychological*
symptoms we must at least consider the questions which feminists
would call political. Such as:

If "women's role" were defined less explicitly in terms of childbearing and physical attractiveness, would the loss of ovarian function
be so traumatic?

If "masculinity" were less a matter of power and performance,
would the diminution of a man's energies be so painfully perceived?
And, conversely, if men were under less pressure to perform, would
there be as much diminution of energies? (This is not only a social
question but a clinical one, for, as already noted, testosterone levels go
down when stress levels go up.)

One learns to approach any statistic in the field with trepidation.
For example, there is this one, often quoted: Three times as many
climacteric-age women as men are hospitalized for treatment of depression. This may suggest that the male climacteric is a pretty
dubious event, after all; or that the hormones wreak far more havoc on
climacteric women than men; or that women are biologically or
psychologically more prone to depression than men; or that behavior
considered benign in men is labeled depressive in women; or simply
that it is more convenient to hospitalize depressed women than depressed men (when *he* is sick, she can take care of him; when *she* is
sick, there is nobody home to take care of her.) Or it could mean that
social sanctions make the climacteric, with all that it implies, much
harder for the woman than for the man: If her value resides primarily

in childbearing, she is finished after menopause; whereas, if his value resides primarily in work, he is still of some use until age 65. (I note here a statistic passed on by Mary Jane Gray, obstetrics and gynecology professor at the University of Vermont, who herself warns that it can be interpreted a dozen different ways: Three times as many Jewish women are hospitalized for menopausal depression as non-Jewish women. All the obvious jokes come to mind, but it hurts to laugh.)

Psychiatrist Robert Seidenberg and obstetrician Howard J. Osofsky, both of the State University of New York Upstate Medical Center, are sufficiently convinced of the social factor in climacteric depression to have written recently: "Sexuality, reproduction and child rearing may be important to both males and females, but they should be choices, and not mandate exclusion of other avenues of fulfillment for women. If such changes are attained, it is likely that menopausal depression will diminish markedly and even vanish almost completely as a clinical entity."

There are persuasive arguments against the societal theory, but none of them seems conclusive. For example, several endocrinologists have pointed out to me what appears to be a sort of ace in the hole: the effects of abrupt and total sex-hormone deprivation. Remove the testes from a healthy, 25-year-old male (or the ovaries from a female) and he may develop the full-blown climacteric syndrome, including depression. Give him testosterone, and the symptoms may be relieved. It seems reasonable to assume a purely hormonal cause and effect. On the other hand, says Mount Sinai's Lear, any assault upon the body can be traumatic, especially one so rife with symbolic content as castration. "There are the physiological symptoms associated with the halt in testosterone production: loss of sex drive and potency, loss of aggressiveness and a general feeling of unwell-being. Add to these the fear that he will be permanently impotent, and of *course* this 25-year-old will be depressed. If testosterone replacement gives him back his energy, his sense of well-being and enables him to function sexually, naturally the depression will be relieved too," Lear says.

"When the hormonal loss is gradual and normal, as in the climacteric years, the realities of his diminishing energy and changing sexual response are undramatic, but they are still realities. How a man handles them depends not only on how he sees himself but also, very much, on how the culture sees him. In a culture where old age brings dignity, honor, status, would we find the same syndrome? I doubt it."

To my knowledge, there are no crosscultural studies of the male climacteric, and none involving our own subcultures. We do not know whether the syndrome would appear, or appear in the same way, given a different set of cultural values. But anthropological observations suggest that it would not.

Anthropologist Margaret Mead says: "It's a question of the order of achievement, and the way it paces biological change. Of course, in primitive societies you don't have long career lines—the men die too young. In our society, depression comes when men realize that they've achieved all they're going to achieve: If a man has made it as first vice-president of a bank, but then the bank merges with another bank, and another fellow becomes first vice-president, then that's the end of *him* . . . it is this sort of thing that happens. For the male these are purely exogenous events, and he seeks exogenous solutions—as in getting a young wife.

"It depends, really, on how old age is viewed. I would expect to find depression among late-middle-age men in societies where the diminutions of aging, such as loss of strength, are important. But if old age means having wisdom and skills that don't require physical strength, that's fine. The Australian aboriginal men, when they grew older, had all the ceremonial wisdom and so got most of the young women, and it isn't reported to have depressed them."

Sol Worth, a professor of visual communications at the University of Pennsylvania and author of the recent book, "Through Navaho Eyes," says: "At age 45, when all most of us have to look forward to is getting knocked off, the Navaho is stepping into a new hierarchy. Now he is a leader. He doesn't have to perform. His children and grandchildren can ride the horses and climb the mountains and be virile. He does other things better, like giving advice and orders. If we're talking about climacteric depression as a biocultural event, it doesn't appear to exist here."

Ultimately, it seems impossible to define the male climacteric except in terms of a kind of layering effect, or perhaps a convergence: a profound and immensely complex interaction of hormonal factors, aging processes, ego strengths and weaknesses, social roles and cultural determinants, all coming together at a time when life is, realistically, no feather bed.

A man who is probably in the throes of the climacteric syndrome (except, perhaps, by Kupperman's definition) told me recently:

I'm 54 years old. Fifteen years ago, if they had told me, "Listen, we can't give you a raise,' I might have said, 'The hell with you guys.

You can take this job and shove it,' and I would have gone somewhere else. But when it happened now . . . where could I go? Who is hiring 54-year-old men these days? I was terribly depressed. It created a whole bunch of complexes I never knew I had. It knocked the hell out of my sex life and everything else."

Probably contained therein is the whole interaction, and probably there can be no sorting out of one layer from another. The hormone-production levels are dropping, the head is balding, the sexual vigor is diminishing, the stress is unending, the children are leaving, the parents are dying, the job horizons are narrowing, the friends are having their first heart attacks; the past floats by in a fog of hopes not realized, opportunities not grasped, women not bedded, potentials not fulfilled, and the future is a confrontation with one's own mortality. So: What causes the male climateric?

∿   ∿   ∿

We don't know what causes the male climacteric, nor are we sure what causes a healthy old age. There are no magic prescriptions for a long healthy life. If we could have, we should have all picked long-living parents and grandparents; heredity probably has much to do with longevity. However, the studies of long-lived people in certain communities, such as those in the Caucasus, seem to show that heredity merely protects us from some diseases rather than causing us to live longer.

Diet has been implicated many times. In rat studies, it was found that the rat's life could be doubled if the diet was so reduced as to retard the rat's maturation. The long-lived people studied by Alexander Leaf had diets that contained half as many calories as is typical in the United States. Fats have already been implicated in the development of arteriosclerosis. Heavy people are more prone to diabetes, and often to bone-breaking falls; their heart has more work to do and may collapse more easily. Eating less, yet more wisely, is one way to help insure health at any age, but especially in adulthood.

Exercise strengthens the heart, keeps the muscle in tone, may retard the formation of cholesterol, and certainly helps people feel more vigorous. But exercise should be part of the life-style, rather than faddish, or something done only on sunny Saturdays. There are many good ways to exercise, but vigorous programs should always take the current body into consideration; for that reason, a doctor's advice is necessary.

Most of the changes associated with aging are not extremely limiting; probably the most important part of biological aging is how we feel about ourselves, and whether we feel we have a part to play in society.

4

human sexuality: dirty old man or sexy senior citizen?

Think about romance. A moonlit night . . . or a bar . . . or a bedroom. Imagine who would be touching, caressing, sighing, and breathing heavily. Probably your images are not of gray-haired ladies and gentlemen reaching out to each other (or to you). Why is this? Why does the "gay young blade" turn into a "dirty old man"? Or will you want to be a sexy senior citizen? What can you expect?

Sex is important to the young, as we all know. It satisfies needs to be touched, to be close physically and emotionally. It feels good and it's fun. Sexual activities help us feel attractive and good about ourselves. For some, the ability to achieve multiple orgasms, or to have intercourse with many different people, or to elicit a proposition provides evidence of success and achievement similar to making a low golf score or winning a legal case. Sexual behavior can be excellent recreation; not much special equipment is necessary; it is an all-weather, all-locale activity which provides excellent exercise. The pleasure afforded to oneself and to the partner can make life glow.

With all these advantages, why limit it to the young? In the past, older people were commonly regarded as asexual. Regardless of private behavior, it was considered poor taste to show public evidence of continued sexual interest and activity. The anticipated loss of this pleasurable activity and this part of the self contributes to the denial of aging: if to grow older is no longer to be sexy, resist.

The image is changing, though slowly. We begin to see, in the popular press and in professional journals, articles about continued sexual activity throughout adulthood. Rubin summarizes the evidence about sexual behavior after forty. We can expect that whatever we know now about sexuality will be revised substantially in the next decades, just as the "marriage manuals" of a decade ago now seem hopelessly inaccurate and quaint. In particular, sexual behavior during the later adult years will be very different for generations now young— if they discover and become comfortable with their own sexuality.

Sex After Forty—and After Seventy

Isadore Rubin, Ph.D

SMASHING A DANGEROUS STEREOTYPE

One of the major contributions of Dr. William H. Masters and Mrs. Virginia E. Johnson has been their detailed laboratory study of the sexual responses of older persons. Their work helps fill the gaps in medical knowledge and clinical experience. It helps break the conspiracy of silence about sexuality in the later years. And it helps destroy the stereotype of "sexless old age," which has done such serious harm to the health and happiness of the aging. Masters and Johnson, it is true, did find important physiological changes in sex response occurring as the years go by. But their major conclusions are unequivocal: "There is no time limit drawn by the advancing years to female sexuality"; and for the male, too, there is, under favorable physical and emotional conditions, "a capacity for sexual performance that frequently may extend beyond the eighty-year age level."

These conclusions are supported by the findings of a growing body of research by other investigators.

In the past, the failure of society to recognize the sexual needs of older people was serious, but not critical. Today, when more than twenty-five million of our population have reached the age of sixty—a figure that is expected to mount to over thirty-one million by 1975— society can hardly afford to maintain the false myths about sexlessness in these years. In the early 1960's, over thirty-five thousand marriages a year took place in which at least one of the partners was sixty-five or older.

These myths are not limited to the years after sixty, although they take much greater hold in these years. For women who are not emotionally prepared for it, the end of menstruation may be a traumatic event. For many of them menstruation has been a badge of femininity and a symbol of youth. As long as it continues they may feel they are still young and attractive in spite of the changes that have taken place over the years. When menstruation ends, writes gynecologist Howard A. Novell, "a woman suddenly has the mirror of life thrust at her and she takes a long, agonizing look and begins a period of marked introspection and usually faulty reappraisal of herself." It is at this vulnerable time in her life that all the folklore related to the menopause comes to bear on some women with great force. One idea is that after the change of life a woman loses her sexual desire and is less capable of functioning sexually than before. This myth, of course, has no anatomical or physiological basis.

Every counselor who deals in any way with sex problems can report many cases of marriages that were brought to the point of disaster because one partner had suddenly decided that the couple was "too old for sex." "I am fifty-eight years old and my wife is fifty-five," wrote one husband to the physician conducting the question and answer column of *Sexology* magazine. "Until about three years ago our sexual life was quite normal, but since that time (contrary to my desires) my wife has not permitted intercourse. Her apathy is even greater since her change of life a year and a half ago. She says I am too old to be so 'foolish' concerning sexual relations and that nobody at this age has sexual desires." "My wife and I are over sixty-five years old but we still like to have sexual intercourse very much," another husband wrote. "Please give us advice in this case. What should we do?"

These examples indicate how older people—unsure about their roles in a new stage of life for which they have been little prepared— reflect the popular ignorance about sexuality. Such attitudes require the authority of the physician to correct them and to dispel the guilt that older couples may have about sexual needs and desires. All too often in the past, however, the physician has had the same ignorance about sex in the later years and has reflected the same guilt feelings about sex. In too many cases an older patient who has sought advice from a physician about waning sex ability and responsiveness is greeted merely with evasive laughter—or with the question, "What do you expect at your age?"

If these attitudes affected only the sex life of older persons, they would still be serious enough. However, they go far beyond this to strike at the whole self-image of the older man and woman, complicating and distorting all their interpersonal reactions in marriage. They have serious effects on the diagnosis of many medical and psychological problems and upon the administration of justice to older persons accused of sex offenses. Not least of all, they have unfortunate effects on the relationships of children and parents thinking of remarriage; the reaction of too many children is, "They ought to know better."

Today, with the benefit of the Masters-Johnson research—added to the surveys of behavior in the later years by the Kinsey investigators, by Drs. Gustave Newman and Claude R. Nichols at Duke University, by urologists at the University of California School of Medicine at San Francisco, by Dr. Joseph T. Freeman in Philadelphia, by *Sexology* magazine, and others—there is no longer any reason for anyone to continue to believe that sex, love, and marriage are the exclusive privileges of youth. The research has clearly established that—under the proper physical and emotional conditions—the capacity to enjoy sex is not lost in the later years but simply slows down gradually, along with other physical capacities.

THE RESEARCH EVIDENCE

A number of other investigators have surveyed the sexual behavior of older persons. Masters and Johnson were the first actually to observe the anatomy and physiology of their sexual response under laboratory conditions. Included in this part of the study were sixty-one menopausal and postmenopausal women (ages forty to seventy-eight) and thirty-nine men (ages fifty-one to eighty-nine). Obviously, these numbers were not large enough to provide biological data of statistical significance and further studies will be required, but they furnished important preliminary information.

When the orgasmic cycles of the women of this group were studied, Masters and Johnson found that generally the intensity of physiologic reaction, and the rapidity and duration of anatomic response to sexual stimulation were reduced with advancing years through all phases of the sexual cycle. That is, the sex flush was more limited and restricted in the older women, there was less lubrication, there was delay in reaction of the clitoris to direct stimulation, reduction of duration in orgasm time, etc. However, they emphasized, they did find "significant sexual capacity and effective sexual performance" in these older women. "The aging human female," they concluded, "is fully capable of sexual performance at orgasmic response levels, particularly if she is exposed to regularity of effective sexual stimulation." They added that there seems to be no physiologic reason why the frequency of sexual expression found satisfactory for the younger woman should not be carried over into the years after the menopause, with no time limit drawn by the advancing years.

As in the female, Masters and Johnson found that in men after fifty the intensity and duration of physical responses during the orgasmic cycle are lessened; particularly after sixty, erection takes much longer, ejaculation lacks the same force and duration, the sex flush is markedly reduced, etc. "There is no question," they state, "that the human male's sexual responsiveness wanes as he ages." However, they add, when regularity of sexual expression is maintained in a sexually stimulative climate within the marriage, a healthy male's capacity for sexual expression could extend beyond the seventies and the eighty-year age level.

Masters' and Johnson's findings that sexual activity continues—though on a reduced scale—into advanced old age in many persons is well substantiated by other research, as is their finding that there is no basis for any physiological effect of menopause on frequency of intercourse for women.

In the Kinsey studies the investigators also found little evidence of any aging in the sexual capacities of women. "Over the years," they reported, "most females become less inhibited and develop an interest in sexual relations which they may then maintain until they are in their fifties or even sixties." In their later years, sexual activity of course depends to a large extent on the desires and capacities of their husbands, who would generally average three or four years older. The responses of the average husband, in contrast to the average wife, drop with age. Thus, many of the younger women reported that they did not wish to have intercourse as often as their husbands, but in the later years of marriage, many of the women expressed the desire to have intercourse more often than their husbands.

As far as males were concerned, the Kinsey investigators did find evidence of a weakening of sexual response with age. Morning erections, for example, which had averaged 4.9 per week in the early years, had dropped to an average of 1.8 at sixty-five and to 0.9 per week at age seventy-five. However, for most males they found that there was no point at which old age suddenly enters the picture. One white male was still averaging seven ejaculations each week at the age of seventy, and an eighty-eight-year-old man and his ninety-year-old wife still continued their sexual life.

In 1959 a group of urologists at the University of California Medical Center at San Francisco reported on their study of 101 men who had come as patients to their outpatient clinics. There was a general decline with age, but sixty-five percent of the men under seventy were still capable of sexual relations. Of the males over seventy, one third of the number were still potent.

In 1960 a report was made by Drs. Gustave Newman and Claude R. Nichols of an investigation into the sexual activity of 250 persons living in the Piedmont area of North Carolina, ranging in age from sixty to ninety-three years of age. They found, out of the 149 persons still married and living with their husbands or wives, that more than half were still sexually active (54 percent). They concluded that "given the conditions of reasonably good health and partners who are physically healthy, elderly persons continue to be sexually active into their seventh, eighth and ninth decades."

This same general finding was reported by Dr. Joseph T. Freeman, who among other things found that by the age of eighty a number of men studied still reported no cessation of desire and some were still potent. Drs. L. M. Bowers, R. R. Cross, Jr. and F. A. Lloyd, who studied veterans applying for a pension, reached the same conclusion.

One of the largest surveys was conducted by *Sexology* magazine, which mailed questionnaires to men over sixty-five who had attained enough eminence in various fields to be listed in *Who's Who in America*. More than eight hundred men answered the series of questions. Of the married men who still had partners, over 70 percent indicated that they still engaged with some regularity in sexual intercourse, most with general satisfaction. Even in the group of 104 men aged seventy-five to ninety-two, almost one-half reported that intercourse was still satisfactory, and six engaged in coitus on the average of about eight times a month.

One interesting survey on the attitudes of women toward the menopause was conducted by Dr. Bernice L. Neugarten and her colleagues of the Committee on Human Development at the University of Chicago. They found that among the women who had not yet gone through the menopause there was a great deal of uncertainty about how the menopause would affect their sex lives, with the youngest group disagreeing most with the view that menopausal women may experience an upsurge of sexual impulse. "I was afraid we couldn't have sexual relations after the menopause," said one woman, "and my husband thought so, too." However, in the group of women who were between the ages of fifty-five and sixty-five, 21 percent of them felt that "after the menopause, a woman is more interested in sex than before."

It should be noted that none of these studies involved a sufficiently large or sufficiently representative group of men or women for the figures to be typical of the average older man or woman. However, all of them do confirm the Masters and Johnson findings that there is no particular stage of life or age that represents a cut-off point for sexual desire, response or ability, even though age does reduce the strength of sexual response.

THE IMPORTANCE
OF REGULARITY

One of the points that Masters and Johnson keep emphasizing in their discussion of the factors necessary for maintaining sexual capacity and effective sexual performance is regularity of sexual performance. This, they say, is essential for both males and females.

As a result of lowered hormone production in the female in the later years, thinning of the vaginal walls and reduced lubrication make intercourse uncomfortable and even painful. However, three women past sixty years of age were repeatedly observed to expand and lubricate the vagina effectively despite obvious senile thinning of the vaginal walls and shrinking of the major labia. These women had maintained regular intercourse once or twice a week for their entire adult lives. On the other hand, women, five to ten years after the end of menstruation, who had intercourse infrequently (once a month or less) and who did not masturbate with regularity had difficulty in accommodating the penis during their rare exposures to intercourse.

Regularity of sexual expression is also the key to sexual responsiveness for the aging male, say Masters and Johnson. With loss of sexual outlet, many aging males report rapid loss of sexual tension and potency. Regularity is important, apparently, not only in the later years but in the earlier years as well.

"The most important factor in the maintenance of effective sexuality for the aging male is consistency of active sexual expression," Masters and Johnson assert. "When the male is stimulated to high sexual output during his formative years and a similar tenor of activity is established for the 31–40-year range, his middle-aged and involutional years usually are marked by constantly recurring physiologic evidence of maintained sexuality. Certainly it is true for the male geriatric sample that those men currently interested in relatively high levels of sexual expression report similar activity levels from their formative years. It does not appear to matter what manner of sexual expression has been employed, as long as high levels of activity were maintained."

This finding, which indicates that there is a close correlation between activity levels in the earlier years and those in the later years, is supported by the findings of the Kinsey research. It does not, of course, prove a cause-and-effect relationship, since it may merely indicate that those with the strongest sex drives had greater sex activity both in the early and later years. But it does effectively demolish one of the great myths about sexual activity that has persisted from ancient days down to the very present—the idea that one can use oneself up sexually and that it is necessary to save oneself for the later years. This myth is connected with the belief that the emission of semen through any kind of sexual activity weakens and debilitates. Many people still believe that each drop of semen emitted in ejaculation is equivalent to the loss of forty drops of blood. Such beliefs are hard to overcome since they go back thousands of years to ancient Chinese, Greek, and Hindu views.

"My husband," writes a woman to a doctor, "has reached the age of sixty-five. He has decided that, in order to ensure a longer life and health, he will no longer engage in sex activity. He is convinced that intercourse and the emission of semen are quite debilitating, particularly in his years." The feeling of this man is not unusual. Dr. Morton

M. Golden reported that many of his patients had the distorted notion that males have a limited number of sperm and were convinced that masturbation had used up their supply of sperm cells and energy. "I have seen patients," he wrote, "who deliberately began a program of abstinence in the fourth decade to postpone the inevitable 'catastrophe of old age.' "

Actually, it is well recognized today that the emission of semen is no more of a loss than the expectoration of saliva. Both are quickly replaced by the body.

The notion that one can prolong sex life by being inactive in the earlier years and less active in the older years is particulary contradicted by the findings of the Kinsey group. They found that at age fifty all the males who had been sexually active in their early adolescence were still sexually capable, with a frequency about 20 percent higher than the males who had begun activity later. "Nearly forty years of maximum activity," they say, "have not yet worn them out physically, physiologically, or psychologically. On the other hand, some of the males (not many), who [began sexual activity in late adolescence] and who have had five years less of sexual activity, are beginning to drop completely out of the picture; and the rates of this group are definitely lower in these older age periods."

There is no question that other leading sexologists agree with Masters and Johnson on the importance of regularity and consistency in maintaining effective sexual functioning. Professor Tadeusz Bilikiewicz of the Medical Academy of Gdansk, Poland, points out that "the most effective way to secure the longest possible functioning of organs is by letting them work continuously and systematically." Hence, far from advising abstinence for those who wish to preserve sexual life, he concludes that the best advice that specialists in aging can give is: "Try to maintain your intellectual and sexual activities as long as possible."

Dr. John F. Oliven, an authority on sexual functioning, has also emphasized regularity of intercourse. Very often in the older years, the sexual life of a couple is disrupted by a more or less prolonged period of abstinence because of surgery or some health reason. Prolonging the period of abstinence longer than is necessary invites certain dangers to the marriage, Dr. Oliven notes. He suggests to doctors that as a general rule, the greatest possible sexual freedom at the earliest possible time compatible with the remedial program should be allowed, or even encouraged.

Thus, authorities are in agreement with Masters' and Johnson's emphasis on the importance of regular sexual performance in helping maintain effective sexual capacity for both men and women.

THE POSTMENOPAUSAL YEARS

One of the problems faced by women in their postmenopausal years is the loss of estrogen brought about as the ovaries reduce their production of hormones. This loss generally begins to manifest itself about five years after the end of menstruation and is quite evident in most of the women who have reached sixty years of age, although there are many individual exceptions. Masters and Johnson note that, as the woman moves through her postmenopausal years, the lining of the vagina becomes very thin and atrophic. Instead of having the thick, ridged pattern characteristic of the vagina when it is receiving considerable estrogen stimulation, the walls of the vagina become tissue-paper-thin and, therefore, cannot protect the structures lying next to the vagina—the urethra and bladder—by absorbing the mechanical irritation of active intercourse. There is also a shortening of both vaginal length and width and a shrinking of the major labia, leading to constriction of the opening of the vagina.

In addition, once the woman is about five years past the menopause, the rate and amount of lubrication production diminish to an obvious degree. This is not true for all women, since Masters and Johnson observed three women over sixty, one as old as seventy-three, who consistently responded to sexual stimulation with rapid production of lubrication typical of women under thirty. All three of these women had very active sex lives throughout their mature years.

Another result of steroid imbalance is that contractions of the uterus, which take place during orgasm at all age levels, now become painful. For some women these contractions are so painful that they seek to avoid orgasm and even intercourse itself.

As a result of these changes, intercourse during the postmenopausal years may be painful in many ways. Some women find penetration and the friction of intercourse painful. Some complain of a burning on urination, which develops from mechanical irritation of the urethra and bladder because of the thrusting movement of the penis. It is not unusual for many to have an urgent need to urinate immediately after intercourse.

Fortunately, today, it is easily possible to make up for any lack of hormone production in the body with adequate hormone-replacement therapy. In some cases, local application of a simple lubricant between the lips of the vulva will relieve the discomfort entirely. If the tissues are very thin and tender, estrogen creams or suppositories applied locally to the vulva and vagina may restore the tissues to normal layers and cure the discomfort within a week or two. In addition, more and more women are being given general replacement therapy to make up for the loss of hormone production by the ovaries.

However, as Masters and Johnson point out, the effect of hormone imbalance on sexual adjustment after the menopause is not the major factor. Sexual performance in many cases depends far more on opportunity for regular intercourse and on numerous emotional factors than it does on hormone balance. Many women develop renewed interest in their husbands and have described a "second honeymoon" during the early fifties as a result of the ending of any fear of pregnancy. In addition, women beyond the years of fifty have resolved most of the problems connected with raising a family, and frequently there is a significant increase in their sexual activity. On the other hand, one must not overlook the fact that many women who have never been too happy about sex during most of their lives find in the menopause or in their advancing years a respectable reason for ending a duty that has always been onerous or distasteful to them.

MAINTAINING MALE RESPONSIVENESS

In their clinical work with older males, Masters and Johnson found six general categories of factors which were responsible for loss of sexual responsiveness during the later years: (1) monotony of a repetitious sexual relationship (usually translated into boredom with the wife); (2) preoccupation with career or economic pursuits; (3) mental or physical fatigue; (4) overindulgence in food or drink; (5) physical and mental infirmities of either the man or his wife; and (6) the "fear of failure."

The problem of monotony, which is probably the single most important factor in the loss of an aging male's sexual interest and responsiveness, has been noted by many others besides Masters and Johnson. Kinsey and his colleagues described it as "psychologic fatigue"—the fact that there is just not as much psychological stimulation in an experience that is repeated without too much novelty or variation with the same partner over an extended period of time.

One factor contributing to this boredom may be the occurrence of many physical and psychological changes—some of them due to solvenly habits developed by a wife as she grows older—which may inhibit or destroy sexual interest or response. This was clearly shown by a study made by Dr. A. L. Wolbarst in the middle 1940's when he studied one hundred consecutive cases of older patients who had come for treatment for "impotence." Dr. Wolbarst found that many of the older patients who considered themselves totally impotent reported that they were not impotent with other women, only with their wives. In some of these cases, the husbands were repelled by physical characteristics, some of which could be corrected by diet, plastic surgery, or other means.

Sexual boredom is more likely to take place if the couple—like most persons in our society—have restricted themselves to a mechanical and repetitious sex life, without variety or novelty to bring new stimulation to it; many have done so because of the no longer accepted view that only certain methods of lovemaking are right and proper, while other methods are degrading and illegitimate.

The practical lesson for married couples that want to maintain their sex lives is an obvious one. "From middle age onward," suggests Maxine Davis, "a wife had better take steps to jolt her husband out of his rut, to use her imagination and experience to bring surprise into their sexual activity. . . . Even though she has been content enough to let the sexual relationship rock agreeably along in a uniform pattern for years, it is never too late—or too soon—to open new doors to adventure and romance."

Of course, it would be wrong to place all the responsibility for weakening sexual response on the wife. In many cases, Masters and Johnson reported, men were so preoccupied with their careers that outside interests were all-consuming, becoming a major deterrent to sexual activity in the home, particularly when communication between husband and wife was poor. For some men over fifty strenuous weekend activity, to which they are generally not accustomed, is enough to reduce their sexual responsiveness. More important is mental exhaustion, perhaps resulting from "a bad day at the office" or from occupational, financial, or personal emergencies.

Excessive consumption of either food or drink also has a tendency to repress sexual feelings; Masters and Johnson found that secondary impotence developing in the late forties or early fifties has a greater connection with excessive drinking than with any other single factor.

It is clear that as men age, they have an increasing number of minor, or in some cases major, physical disabilities, each of which may in some way lower sexual responsiveness. When the wife is affected, it may restrict opportunities for sexual intercourse for the husband, often putting an end to sexual life altogether. With the loss of sexual outlet, as we have seen, many aging males report a rapid loss of sexual responsiveness and ability.

Obviously, any acute illness is accepted without question by both husband and wife. However, there are many cases where couples are given inadequate advice by their physicians and as a result unnecessarily abstain from sexual relations out of ignorance or fear. This was dramatically shown by a report given by three heart specialists at the 1964 annual convention of the American College of Cardiology. These physicians questioned a number of men who had had heart attacks, asking them about their sexual activity after the attacks. The heart attacks had occurred from one to nine years before the interviews. The physicians found that only about a third of these men resumed their normal pattern of sexual activity, and that 10 percent had become completely impotent.

The most significant thing about these results is this: the pattern of sexual activity following the heart attack had *no relation* either to the age of the men or to the severity of the attack. It depended entirely on the attitudes of the men involved. Practically none of the men had received from his physician any detailed and specific advice about sexual activity. One third of the men reported that their doctors had given them only vague advice about sexual intercourse. The other two thirds had received no guidance at all. As a result, each patient had to make his own decision.

Today, heart specialists recognize that, under their advice, men may engage in sexual intercourse under carefully regulated conditions after heart attacks, and that the tension generated by sexual frustration may be more harmful than the tension generated by sedate and relaxed intercourse. In their laboratory research, Masters and Johnson checked heart, blood pressure, and pulse rates of males and females during intercourse, and hope to provide in the near future more complete data to guide physicians in their treatment of heart patients.

Dr. Alex L. Finkle and his colleagues at the University of California Medical Center at San Francisco have also pointed to the responsibility of the physician in contributing to the impotence of males who have undergone prostate surgery in the older years. After most types of prostate surgery, sexual ability is present in many of those males who were capable prior to surgery. Sometimes, however, the attitude of the physician may help suppress sexual activity, or the physician may even cause impotence by predicting it.

Few factors play as important a part in bringing about impotence as does the fear of failure. A temporary loss of desire or a temporary failure of potency may occur at any age. In the earlier years, however, a temporary failure may be taken more or less in stride, although even here it may strike quite a blow at the male ego. When it occurs in the later years, when a certain decline has already occurred, it may convince the male that "this is it"—that he has reached the end of his sex life. When he embarks on subsequent sexual trials—determined to succeed, but beginning to doubt whether he can—the atmosphere is not conducive to success. Often, after a period this uncertainty and fear, he may stop attempting intercourse at all because he "knows" he will fail. He often comes to regard himself as totally impotent, feeling that his situation is next to hopeless. Yet it has been demonstrated that once the fear has been overcome, the situation is far from hopeless.

Invariably, the attention of men who consider themselves impotent turns to such possible solutions as hormones, aphrodisiacs, and, as a final resort, artificial devices to satisfy their wives.

It is still a controversial question as to whether or not males go through a physiological readjustment comparable with the female climacteric, or menopause, when there is a sharp decline in the production of hormones. The output of the male hormone (androgen) declines steadily but very slowly in most men until they reach the age of sixty, and remains relatively constant thereafter. Even among octogenarians, individuals with urinary excretion of hormones within the normal range of young adults have been found.

However, some men do show signs and symptoms so similar to the female's that they have been regarded by many physicians as experiencing a climacteric, usually about ten to fifteen years later than in women. One of the symptoms of this may be a sudden *increase* in sexuality—caused by the fear of a loss of potency and the need of the male to demonstrate to himself that he is "still the man he once was."

Where androgen deficiency exists in aging males, administration of sex hormone may help to restore sexual interest and ability. However, Masters and Johnson note their clinical impression that the obvious elevation of eroticism that may occur after the administration of hormones is not a direct effect of steroid replacement, but rather a secondary result of the obvious improvement in total body economy and of a renewed sense of well-being.

Also, one cannot discount the effect of the power of suggestion, as is clearly demonstrated by this story. When the synthetic male sex hormone testosterone was first introduced at the Johns Hopkins Hospital in Baltimore, a fifty-five-year-old technician observed the remarkable improvement that often seemed to occur and asked the doctors to give him an injection in order to help him revive his waning sexual power. After he got the injection, he reported to the hospital in high spirits convinced that his youthful vigor had been restored. Each time he requested an injection thereafter, he was given one of sterile oil, taken from a bottle labeled "testosterone." On each occasion, the technician happily reported that the results of the later injections were just as effective as the first.

This power of suggestion operates in the case of many foods and drinks that have traditionally been described as aphrodisiacs. Their effect is purely psychological, but since sexual functioning has so great a psychological component, they all seem to be quite effective.

There is another group of so-called aphrodisiacs that operate in a different manner. Some of them—like herbs and spices—may irritate the lining of the genital and urinary tract as they are being voided; the irritation may produce sensations resembling sexual arousal, bringing about a vague genital urge and a reflex erection. Some substances —like the famous irritant *cantharides,* known popularly as "Spanish fly"—are powerful corrosive poisons, which can cause serious destruction of tissue and sometimes death.

According to the Kinsey investigators, "good health, sufficient exercise, and plenty of sleep still remain the most effective of the aphrodisiacs known to man."

Judging from the requests that many doctors doing sex counseling receive, there is a wide demand for mechanical devices to aid the aging and impotent male. These devices take many forms, including extensions, splints, suction devices, and clasps. Unfortunately, so little attention has been paid to these devices by the medical profession that few doctors have enough experience to offer a well-qualified opinion. Those who have had experience report that in a few cases reasonable satisfaction has been obtained, but that in most cases the device was soon discarded because the male had so little sensation from it and the wife so often found it unromantic or ridiculed it. One leading marriage counselor has pointed out that a simple rubber band placed around the base of the penis has helped maintain an erection and has been less objectionable than expensive devices.

One final word should be said about the man or woman who does not have an available partner but still has sexual needs. Most persons are accustomed to think of masturbation as a childish activity which is outgrown once the individual reaches adulthood. Actually, every study of older people has shown that large numbers of them engage in masturbation as an alternative method of gaining release from sexual tension, though some of them feel disturbed because they feel there is something wrong for persons of their age to engage in this practice. "It is to be hoped," said Lester W. Dearborn, a pioneering marriage counselor, "that those interested in the field of geriatrics will take into consideration the sexual needs of the aging and encourage them to accept masturbation as a perfectly valid outlet when there is a need and other means of gratification are not available."   ⌣

⌣   ⌣   ⌣

As Rubin points out, aging men and women differ in sexual patterns no less than do younger men and women. How can we account for these differences?

Sexual behavior is shaped from infancy by practices of the culture and the family. There is probably no sexual practice imaginable which has not been considered acceptable by some people at some point; each culture selects some practices as "normal" and calls others "deviant" or "abnormal." The practices accepted as normal vary enough from culture to culture to demonstrate there is nothing biologically given in any particular practice. However, each of us begins to learn very early in life what it means to be sexual in our particular culture. We learn by observing our mother's reaction to a pat on the fanny from our father; we learn from the hesitation, horror, or ease with which our parents treat early masturbation and questions about sex; we learn from the way we are handled that touching and caressing are forms of communication and pleasure or that touch is shameful, particularly on our "private parts." We also learn from advertising, from church, and from our peers.

The attitudes toward sex and our own sexuality that are formed in childhood remain embedded in the subconscious, even if we consciously change our views as adults. The 45-year-old man who grew up believing sex to be dirty and shameful may think he would like to be a "swinger" before it's too late; he may long to be free to enjoy sexuality, and may linger over pornography secretly. But affairs will likely involve a mixture of joy and guilt that can lead to impotence, despair, and anger at himself over his own inexplicable feelings. If we wish to understand the sexual attitudes and behavior of older adults, we should look to the values they acquired in their youth; if they "learned" that wrinkles and menopause mark the end of sexuality, it should not surprise us that as elderly people they are uninterested; nor should we feel compelled to change them, for sexual crusades are hardly appropriate. However, it means that the fate of our own sexuality is also subject to our beliefs; if we see sexuality as valuable and natural at every age, we will feel comfortable with and able to enjoy it as we grow older.

Women and men have traditionally held different views about sexuality. The popular mythology has assigned women the task of sexual control—a useful and realistic task considering the perils of pregnancy before birth-control technology. Adolescent girls were told to keep the hot-blooded young males in line and out of their pants; "giving yourself" should be reserved for the man with a commitment to take the consequences, usually in the form of a marriage proposal. Sexuality control, of their own and the male's feelings, may have been functional for young girls, but it is not appropriate for women.

The denial of sexual feelings and urges throughout childhood and adolescence means that the young woman has not explored her own body to find what feels good. If she does not know herself, it is difficult for her to help her lover be effective. After years of close control, sexual feelings are not suddenly free and enjoyable simply because marriage vows have been spoken.

Several studies have shown that sexual activity for most women is tied to the availability of a sexual partner they feel is appropriate; unlike men, they have not used casual encounters and masturbation as sexual activities. For most women, and many men, emotional commitment is a very important aspect of sexuality. If they lose their regular partner through divorce, death, lack of interest, impotence, or infidelity, few women will actively seek out a man for a sexual partner. Thus, the chances have been good that women, as they got older, would be left without a sexually capable partner—and their heterosexual activity would thus decline.

Until very recently, women have not become sexually "free" until their early thirties—if then. By that time, most have married, have had children and thus "proven" their femininity, and have gained some confidence from years of experience. They then begin to discover their own bodies. Kinsey reports orgasmic frequency peaking in the early thirties for women. Unfortunately, men often begin withdrawing from sexual activity in middle age as they become increasingly involved in career building; problems can arise as the man's withdrawal occurs at the same time as the woman's increasing interest. We can expect changes in these patterns as women focus on their own sexual fulfillment rather than defining their sexuality as a service to their partner. It seems likely that a generation of men and women who have learned to accept full sexuality as a life-long treat, not bound to age or body appearance, will have many fewer sexual problems than those evident today.

Women are increasingly experiencing other women as good friends; it seems reasonable that sexual intimacy may become a part of that friendship. We may find, particularly in the later years, that biological sex is not the most important characteristic in choosing a partner with whom we can share sensual pleasures.

Sexuality is only one of many areas of human functioning, and for most people it is not a central concern. Unlike eating and breathing, no one has ever died from lack of sexual activity—or from excess. There is no particular reason to recommend sexual activity for older people unless they enjoy it, but there are good reasons for removing embarrassment, shame, guilt, or ridicule from varied sexual expression at any age.

5

parents and children: showdown at generation gap

When we were children, we spoke as children; when we were grown, we put away childish things. We all grow up as creatures of our times and our view of the world is shaped by social events. We also grow up as members of a family, and its influence remains profound. What are predictable changes as we grow from child to adult, and watch in turn our children mature into adulthood?

FAMILY RELATIONSHIPS

Family can include many or few; sometimes, like the Biblical loaves and fishes, it expands to meet the occasion. I shall include all individuals in the family who have a significant relationship with our central person; obviously, one person may include his second cousin, twice removed, when he thinks of his family, and another person may have little interaction with any kin except her mother. Our definition must remain flexible when considering predictable changes in family relationships from middle age on. For our purposes, we shall consider these relationships from the perspective of a middle-aged person; it is virtually impossible to consider family role changes in the abstract since complex multiple family roles are common.

Generally, we have a very inadequate kinship terminology for considering family relationships. Unlike some cultures, we have no terms that precisely indicate our blood relationship to one another.

We call sisters of both parents *aunt,* my husband's sisters and my brother's wives are called *sisters-in-law,* and we group many into the class of *cousin.* The kinship terms of our language indicate that we place more emphasis on immediate family (parents, grandparents, children, grandchildren, and siblings) than more distant kin.

It is important to know which relatives are "family" because family relationships have traditionally provided a form of social insurance in old age. Ties formed during a lifetime provide security against other losses. The aid may not be financial (in modern societies, as Cowgill points out, it often is not), but the family relationships often involve reciprocal helping patterns among generations. For example, the old mother can count on her daughter to telephone, write letters, perhaps run errands, and include her in family celebrations.

However, our family relationships are becoming enormously complex, as divorce, remarriage, and multiple sets of children become more common. The advice columns have many letters asking who should fill a traditional role when there are several possibilities: should the biological father or the stepfather of the last fifteen years act as father of the bride? And, if there are two persons who can fill the social role, the relationship with each of them is likely to be altered. The middle-aged daughter with four surviving "mothers"—her biological mother, stepmother, mother-in-law, and stepmother-in-law—would probably feel inadequate to deal with their aging problems and to provide adequate care and financial support. The middle-aged daughter with one surviving mother and several brothers and sisters might feel pleased and able to share the care of her elderly mother.

Parents. Parents must change their relationship with their child, to prepare him for eventual independence. During adolescence, parents as well as children often have difficulty reworking their relationship. The parents are uncertain when the teen-ager is an adult and when a child; the teen-ager is no more consistent. As the adolescent children leave home, the parents are faced with an emptied house, space in the refrigerator, extra bedrooms, and the loss of one organizing focus. Most parents organize the household at least partially around children. When they are gone, there is often great relief and a renewed sense of freedom—mixed with a sense of uncertainty about how to arrange their greater freedom.

The time of the "empty nest" is stereotypically seen as a crisis period, particularly for women. Mothers are portrayed as bereft of their only meaningful activity, sinking to despair, and finding comfort only in alcohol or frantic volunteerism. The stereotype is not very accurate. Most parents find the empty-nest period promising—a period of greater leisure, financial resources, and relief at having the major child-rearing responsibilities lifted. As one woman said:[1]

> I feel my job with them is done. I don't have to discipline them any more, it's their problem. . . . I hope I can always be a mother, but we'll treat each other as adults. I have a much more relaxed feeling now.

Marjorie Fisk Lowenthal and her colleagues interviewed twenty-seven men and twenty-seven women whose youngest child was about to graduate from high school. They found that neither men nor women singled out the departure of the youngest child as a current problem. One man came the closest to having an "empty nest crisis," but even he was not extreme. Two fathers wished they had had their children earlier and that they were already out on their own. One said:

> I wish now that my children were older, and already out of the house and living their own lives. I would like to be rid of that particular responsibility. I would like to have the accomplishment of raising my children, but also to be discharged of the responsibility of maintaining them. . . . I would prefer that [my son] had already been able to take care of himself a few years earlier, so that I would be able to enjoy my last years at work and also my retirement without being responsible for him.[2]

Nearly half of the respondents in the Lowenthal study listed children or "family" as current satisfactions, or as the things they were most proud of or satisfied with.

Some women *are* very disturbed by the departure of their children. As Pauline Bart points out, these disturbed women tend to be those who have no meaningful occupation or identity other than "Mother." When they no longer have this as an active role, they feel worthless and depressed, and they may end up in psychiatric hospitals.

[1] Marjorie Fisk Lowenthal and David Chiraboga, "Transition to the Empty Nest: Crisis, Challenge, or Relief?" *Archives of General Psychiatry,* January, 1972, V. 26, 8–14.
[2] *Ibid.,* p. 9.

Depression in Middle-Aged Women

Pauline Bart

While some women (such as those studied by Bernice Neugarten and her students) find middle age no more difficult than other life-cycle stages, and some enjoy no longer having to mediate between their children and their husband, the depressed women I studied presented quite a different picture. They had existential suffering; they had to confront the fact that their life pattern was meaningless. They had been super-housewives, super-wives and super-mothers. They had "sacrificed," but martyrs always expect a payoff sometime. And these depressed women learned that there was no payoff because there was no justice. They were thrown back on their own resources, but they had no resources apart from their wife and mother role. They had no selves, nothing to be proud of except their children. Rather than being stock comedy "Jewish Mother" figures, they should be considered as much casualties of our culture as are the children in Harlem whose IQ scores decline with each additional year in school.

Why is it that one woman whose son has been "launched" says, "I don't feel as if I've lost a son; I feel as if I've gained a den," while another thinks the worst thing that ever happened to her was

> when I had to break up and be by myself, and be alone, and I'm just ——I really feel that I'm not only not loved but not even liked sometimes by my own children . . . they could respect me. If——if they can't say good things why should they, why should they feel better when they hurt my feelings, and make me cry, and then call me a crybaby, or tell me that I——I ought to know better or something like that. My worst thing is that I'm alone, I'm not wanted, nobody interests themselves in me . . . nobody cares.

The best times of her life were when she was pregnant and when her children were babies.

We all lose roles throughout our lives, but when we are young there are new roles to replace the old ones and rites of passage to ease the transition. But as we age there usually are not such new roles and there are few rites of passage. There is no Bar Mitzvah for menopause.

I researched the women in three ways. First I used the Human Relations Area Files to study menopause. I learned that menopause is not generally reported as a problem, and that in most societies, particularly those in which there are institutionalized grandmother and mother-in-law roles, women's status goes up. These data suggest that hormones are not the major cause of the difficulties, because if they were, then the problem would be present cross-culturally.

After I completed this cross-cultural study of the roles available to women after childbearing ceased, I examined the records of 533 women between the ages of forty and fifty-nine who had had no previous hospitalization for mental illness. I used five hospitals, ranging from an upper-class private hospital to the two state hospitals that served people from Los Angeles County. I compared women who had been diagnosed "depressed" (using the following diagnoses: involutional depression, psychotic depression, neurotic depression, manic-depressive depressed) with women who had other functional (non-organic) diagnoses.

Next, I conducted twenty intensive interviews at two hospitals to obtain information unavailable from the patient's records, to give the women questionnaires used in studies with "normal" middle-aged women, and to administer the Projective Biography Test—a test consisting of sixteen pictures showing women at different stages in their life cycle and in different roles. These interviews provided an especially rich source of information. I did not read their charts until after the interviews so as not to have my perception affected by psychiatrists' or social workers' evaluations.

I learned that role loss is associated with depression; middle-aged depressed women are more likely to have suffered maternal role loss than nondepressed women. Because we are symbolic creatures in which the past and future are ever present, even impending role loss can bring on depression.

Certain roles appear to be structurally conducive to increasing the effect of the loss of their roles. Women who have overprotective or overinvolved relationships with their children are more likely to suffer depression in their postparental period than women who do not have such relationships. Housewives have a higher rate of depression than women working outside the home. Not only do housewives have more opportunity than women in the labor force to invest themselves completely in their children, but the housewife role is cut down once there are fewer people for whom to shop, cook and clean. Middle-class housewives have a higher rate of depression than working-class housewives, but working-class housewives are more likely to be depressed than working-class women in the labor force.

Depression among middle-aged women with maternal loss is related to the family structure and typical interactive patterns of the ethnic groups to which they belong. When ethnic groups are compared, Jews have the highest rate of depression, Anglos an intermediate rate, and blacks the lowest rate. Since in the traditional Jewish family the most important tie is between the mother and the children and the mother identifies very closely with her children, the larger rate of depression among Jewish women in middle age when their children leave is not surprising. Jewish women are roughly twice as likely to be diagnosed depressed than non-Jewish women; in addition there was a higher ratio of depression to other mental illness among Jewish women than among nonJewish women.

However, when family interactive patterns are controlled, that is, when you compare *all* women who have overprotective or overinvolved relationships with their children, the difference between Jews and non-Jews sharply diminish. Although the data show that overprotection or overinvolvement with children is much more common among Jews than among non-Jews, it is clear that you don't have to be Jewish to be a Jewish mother. For example, one divorced black woman, who had a hysterectomy, went into a depression when her daughter, her only child, moved to Oregon; the depression lifted when she went to Oregon for a visit, and recurred when she returned to Los Angeles.

In middle age it is necessary to be flexible so that new roles can be assumed. The mother role, "helping my children," is most frequently ranked first or second, although only one of the seven women whose children were all home ranked it first, and one ranked it second. Since it is difficult to help children who are no longer home, women who value this behavior more than any other are in trouble; they are frustrated in behaving in the way that is most important to them. Items that were not chosen are as interesting as those that were; only one woman ranked "helping my parents" first. Her hospitalization followed her mother's move to Chicago after she had remodeled her apartment so that her mother could live with her. No woman listed "being a sexual partner to my husband" first, and only one woman listed it second. Three married women did not include it in their ranking, indicating its lack of importance—or their embarrassment or rejection of this role. It is apparent that although eight of the women were in the labor force, occupational role was not important to them; three did not even list it. In short, the women view as important precisely the roles of housemaker and mother that become constrained as the women age. Conversely, they do not consider as important the roles that could be expanded at this time: the sexual-partner role, the occupational role, and the organizational role (taking part in church, club, and community activities.)

A typical example is the following:

> I'm glad that God gave me . . . the privilege of being a mother . . . and I loved them. In fact, I wrapped my love so much around them. . . . I'm grateful to my husband since if it wasn't for him, there wouldn't be the children. They were my whole life. . . . My whole life was that because I had no life with my husband, the children should make me happy . . . but it never worked out.

I will close with a poem I wrote, a Mother's Day Poem for the Depressed Middle Aged Women I Studied:

> "M" is for her menopausal problems.
> "O" is for her "masochistic" needs.
> "T" is for her terror as she ages.
> "H" is for the help for which she pleads.
> "E" is for the emptiness her life is.
> "R" is for the roles that she has lost
> Put them all together they spell MOTHER
> The one the culture's double-crossed.

The challenge of "releasing" mature children is one of the predictable issues of growing older as a parent. This challenge can be met in varied ways, as Lowenthal and Bart point out. It might be the better part of wisdom to consider, while still young, the place that parenthood will have in each of our lives. For those who have many interests and ways to feel important, needed, and competent, the empty nest can be a transition period to focus on other rewarding pursuits.

The empty nest would also be made an easier time if we made

certain revisions in the way work is structured. It is difficult for women who wish to work part time while children are young to find jobs that are suited to their education and training, pay reasonably, and have the flexible hours necessary. Ideally, part-time work should be available in all fields, so that parents can remain involved in building a career. The transition from full-time homemaker/mother to full-time worker does not need to be so abrupt.

As we change the socialization of boys and girls to emphasize planning activities for a long life, the transition of the empty nest will become easier. When females are brought up to expect to work, they will take career preparation more seriously and will be more likely to remain involved outside the home while raising children.

It is a challenge to establish an adult parent-child relationship. As adults live longer, the middle-aged parent will have as many years to enjoy his adult child as he has to raise him. As any parent realizes, it is difficult to give up parenting the person you have watched over since birth; images of the first step, the scraped knee, the adolescent acne, intrude on visions of the child as an adult.

The new relationship may not be as difficult as anticipated, however; the "generation gap" is often more feared than real. While each generation forms attitudes and habits peculiar to its own experiences in growing up, there are many areas where family influences are stronger than age differences. Thus, adult children often share the same basic beliefs, values, and customs of their parents. "Radical" young people seem to have parents who were the radicals of their generation, and politically conservative parents tend to have children who are also relatively conservative. The "showdown at generation gap," even in adolescence, may be more over hair length and musical preferences than over basic beliefs in individual responsibility.[3] The continuity between generations makes it easier to maintain satisfying friendly relations between adult children, their parents, and grandparents.

Grandparenthood. Becoming a grandparent introduces a new social role. We do not have clearly defined roles for grandparents in our culture, although there seem to be several "styles" of grandparenting. Some grandparents play a substitute-parent role, caring for grandchildren on a daily basis while parents are working. Some see grand-

---

[3] Large-scale research on three-generation families at the Andrus Gerontology Center, University of Southern California, will provide more precise answers to the "generation gap" questions.

children as a chance to enjoy limited contacts with children without worrying about discipline and total responsibility. Others interact infrequently and mostly during ritual occasions such as graduations, confirmations, and birthdays.[4]

The following perspective on "What Is a Grandma?" was written by a West Hartford third-grader in response to a school assignment.

What Is a Grandma?

A Grandma is a lady who has no children of her own, so she likes other people's little boys and girls.

A Grandfather is a man Grandmother. He goes for walks with the boys and they talk about fishing and things like that.

Grandmas don't have to do anything except be there. They're so old they shouldn't play hard. It is enough if they drive us to the supermarket where the pretend horse is and have lots of dimes ready.

Or if they take us for walks, they should slow down past things like pretty leaves or caterpillars. And they should never say, "Hurry up!"

Usually they are fat, but not too fat. They wear glasses and funny underwear. They can take their teeth and gums off.

They don't have to be smart, only answer questions like why dogs hate cats, and how come God isn't married.

They don't talk baby talk like visitors do because it is hard to understand.

When they read to us they don't skip words and they don't mind if it is the same story.

Grandmas are the only grownups who have got time—so everybody should have a Grandmother especially if you don't have television.

Becoming a grandparent has traditionally been seen as a sign of aging. In earlier times this was probably a more realistic sign of old age than now. The life span was shorter and the grandparent probably *was* biologically older and nearer to death than now. Grandparenthood today comes in middle age, seldom in old age, and men and women are still fully involved in other activities. As we extend the life span and middle age particularly, perhaps great-grandparenthood will assume the meaning of grandparenthood.

Some individuals do see grandparenthood as signaling the beginning of the end, and are reluctant to admit their new role to anyone. Others, less fearful of aging, welcome the first grandchild as a ticket of admission to a special group (SOGPIP—silly old grandma with pic-

4 Bernice Neugarten and Karol Weinstein, "The Changing American Grandparent," *Journal of Marriage and the Family*, V. 26(2), May, 1964.

tures in purse); they also take pleasure in the evidence of continued immortality through the family.

Margaret Mead reflects about being a grandmother, combining personal experiences and anthropological perspectives. It is clear that she, like many grandmothers, relives her own early years of mothering her daughter—though the prudent grandmother does not share all this remembering with her daughter. The continuity of life is precious: "In the presence of grandparents and grandchild, past and future merge into the present." She also sees her granddaughter as providing her with special opportunities for personal growth and rediscovery of the world: "The known and loved particular child makes it possible for me to understand better and care more about all children." She pleads for more access of grandparents and grandchildren to one another so that each of us may be completely human.

On Being a Grandmother

Margaret Mead

As the years went by, I had carefully not let myself hope that I would have grandchildren, as I knew before Catherine had children I would be old enough to be a great-grandmother. Great-grandmotherhood is something we do not think of as a likely possibility of the human condition, even now when it is becoming more common.

But I did think how delightful it would be, if it happened, to see my daughter with a child. . . . Thinking back to my grandmother and my mother and the kind of mother I had tried to be and remembering all the different kinds of mothering people who had cared for my daughter in her childhood—her English nanny, her lovely young aunt Mary, and her devoted godmother, Aunt Marie, who brought in the generation of my grandmother's day when people respected heirlooms and passed their dolls on from generation to generation—I wondered

From *Blackberry Winter*, by Margaret Mead. © 1972 by Margaret Mead. Reprinted by permission of the William Morrow & Company, Inc., and Angus & Robertson, Ltd.

what kind of child my daughter would have and what kind of mother she would be.

When the news came that Sevanne Margaret was born, I suddenly realized that through no act of my own I had become biologically related to a new human being. This was one thing that had never come up in discussions of grandparenthood and had never before occurred to me. In many primitive societies grandparents and grandchildren are aligned together. A child who has to treat his father with extreme respect may joke with his grandfather and playfully call his grandmother "wife." The tag that grandparents and grandchildren get along so well because they have a common enemy is explicitly faced in many societies. In our own society the point most often made is that grandparents can enjoy their grandchildren because they have no responsibility for them, they do not have to discipline them and they lack the guilt and anxiety of parenthood. All these things were familiar. But I had never thought how strange it was to be involved at a distance in the birth of a biological descendant.

I always have been acutely aware of the way one life touches another—of the ties between myself and those whom I have never met, but who read *Coming of Age in Samoa* and decided to become anthropologists. From the time of my childhood I was able to conceive of my relationship to all my forebears, some of whose genes I carry, both those I did not know even by name and those who helped to bring me up, particularly my paternal grandmother. But the idea that as a grandparent one was dealing with action at a distance—that somewhere, miles away, a series of events occurred that changed one's own status forever—I had not thought of that and I found it very odd.

I felt something like the shock that must be felt by those who have lived all their lives secure in their citizenship in the nation of their birth and who then, suddenly, by the arbitrary act of some tyrannical government, find that they are disenfranchised—as happened to the old aristocracy in Russia after the revolution, to the Jews in Germany in the 1930's, and to the Turkish Armenians in Turkey. But of course what happened to me was not an arbitrary denial of something I had regarded as irreversibly given, but rather an arbitrary confirmation of a state which I felt that I myself had done nothing to bring about. Scientists and philosophers have speculated at length about the sources of man's belief that he is a creature with a future life or, somewhat less commonly, with a life that preceded his life on earth. Speculation may be the only kind of answer that is possible, but I would now add to the speculations that are more familiar another of my own: the extraordinary sense of having been transformed not by any act of one's own but by the act of one's child.

Then, as a new grandmother, I began both to relive my own daughter's infancy and to observe the manifestations of temperament in the tiny creature who was called Vanni—to note how she learned to ignore the noisy carpentry as the house was finished around her but was so sensitive to changes in the human voice that her mother had to keep low background music playing to mask the change in tone of voice that took place when someone who had been speaking then answered the telephone. I remarked how she responded to pattern in the brightly colored chintzes and the mobiles that had been prepared for her. I showed the movies of Cathy's birth and early childhood, to which my daughter commented, "I think my baby is brighter"—or prettier, or livelier—"than your baby!"

However, I felt none of the much trumpeted freedom from responsibility that grandparents are supposed to feel. Actually, it seems to me that the obligation to be a resource but not an interference is just as preoccupying as the attention one gives to one's own children. I think we do not allow sufficiently for the obligation we lay on grandparents to keep themselves out of the picture—not to interfere, not to spoil, not to insist, not to intrude—and, if they are old and frail, to go and live apart in an old people's home (by whatever name it may be called) and to say that they are happy when, once in a great while, their children bring their grandchildren to visit them.

Most American grandparents are supported in their laborious insistence on not being a nuisance by the way they felt toward their own parents and by the fierceness with which, as young adults, they resented interference by their parents and grandparents. But I had none of this. I had loved my grandmother and I had valued the way my mother nursed and loved her children. My only complaint when I took Cathy home as a baby was that Mother could not remember as much as I would have liked about the things it was useful to know. And I had quite gladly shared my baby with her nurse and with my closest friends.

Catherine learned, as I had learned, that having a baby teaches you a great deal about mothers, however much you already may know about babies.

Sevanne Margaret, called Vanni, is the child her parents wanted. At birth she was petite and she has remained petite, so that people still respond to her as if she were almost weightless. She has a beautiful head of dark curling hair, her eyes dance with repsonsiveness, her laughter echoes her mother's laughter, and her confidence matches her father's as he tosses her, easily and surely, up in the air.

Last week I took her, now a little more than two years old, to the aquarium in Boston. It is a place that may well be a nightmare to many small children, for it is dark and crowded with shouting, rushing older children, and intermittently lights flash and loudspeakers boom. But Vanni, dressed in bright green, her astonishing hair blowing out behind her, fearlessly darted here and there, her progress interrupted only by the guards who picked her up to show her fish swimming too high for her eyes to see. She is already making a place for herself and in her minuteness and responsiveness evokes delight and response from others.

And I wonder again about special privilege. I think we shall continue to value diversity and to believe that the family—perhaps more widely assisted by grandparents, aunts and uncles, neighbors and friends and supplemented by more varied experience in other settings —provides the context in which children are best reared to become full human beings. But how then are we to deal with the special privilege that is conferred on a child simply by being the child its parents wanted, which in turn sets the stage for becoming a person other people, too, will think they want?

There are some changes that can be made. In a very few years parents will be able to decide, in advance, the sex of the child they want, so that every child will be the desired son or daughter. Then, for the first time, every girl will know that she was chosen by her parents and is not, as so often has happened, the by-product of a search for boys. The kings and queens in the fairy tales that Catherine wrote as a child had daughters, and within the complexities of the Armenian tradition about the role of the first-born, Barkev's elder brother already had a son. Among Armenians, "The Princess and the Pea" is a favorite fairy tale—a story about a princess who is so light and delicate that she feels the pea through a pile of mattresses, but a princess who is also ready to ride her own horse through the steepest and most dangerous mountain passes.

The whole dilemma of humanity—to yield to and glory in the characteristics we share with other living creatures or, alternatively, to work at and glory in our capacity to transcend our creatureliness—is summed up in the acceptance of the biological child, however different it may be from the parents' dream of a child, and in the dignity and responsibility of those who, forgoing personal creativity, make a full and conscious choice of a child to bring up as their own.

But when all this comes about and the beliefs about such choices are expressed in ritual and art, people still will be faced—parents, real and adoptive, still will be faced—with the extraordinary unevenness, the uncontrollable inequalities of the kind of child that any baby, adopted or biologically one's own, turns out to be. It is true that parents play a considerable role in this. Catherine is a laughing, delighted, imaginative mother, and she gives her child, as she was given, the gift of complete attention. It is true that identical twins, one adopted by a smiling and open mother and the other by a mother who is dour and sour, will respond to the very different behavior of those two mothers. But there is still the possibility that a more smiling baby would have made the dour mother smile and that a fretful, unresponsive baby might have made the smiling mother fretful and anxious.

Watching Vanni, I can see her mother's childhood reflected and intensified in many ways. She is very daring, but also very cautious. Just as her mother used to test every branch when she climbed a tall tree, so Vanni, learning to walk, measured the distance between table and chair. If the distance was too great, she dropped down to creep, but if she could just make it, she walked. She has her mother's reasonableness. If you can explain why you are asking something, she will accede —especially if you give her a part in the action. "Help" and "self"— meaning "I will do it myself"—are important words in her vocabulary. She also has her mother's tendency to dream out something without telling anyone what it is, and when the unwitting adult turns down a different path or enters a door first instead of last, she will burst into tears. Her dark eyes, inherited from her father, flash with some of the intensity that made my grandmother look so much fiercer than I ever did. My responses to her are compounded of my responses to the particularities of my own younger brother and sisters, of my own daughter, of all the babies I have held and cared for, and of all the babies I have observed and studied.

I discovered when I had a child of my own that I had become a biased observer of small children. Instead of looking at them with affectionate but nonpartisan eyes, I saw each of them as older or younger, bigger or smaller, more or less graceful, intelligent, or skilled than my own child. This troubled me. I felt that I learned a great deal about mothers by being one, but that I had become in some way a less objective observer of children. If I think of myself as a scientific observer of children, I would still say that this is true, that being a mother or a grandmother introduces a definite observational bias into descriptions of children of the same age as the child one sees most of from day to day.

But if I think of myself not as a professional student of childhood but simply as a human being, then it seems to me that the effect of my daughter and granddaugher on my view of children—and the world— has to be described quite differently. Instead of a bias that must be compensated for, I have acquired a special and perhaps transient sensitivity. It is as if the child to whom one is bound by greater knowledge and the particularity of love were illuminated and carried a halo of light into any group of children. When Vanni is present, I see the children around her with greater clarity; when she is not there, I visualize two-year-olds—all the two-year-olds I have ever known—with new comprehension. I see their faces more clearly. I understand again, or anew, how they formed their first words. I grasp the meaning of puckered eyebrows, a tensed hand, or a light flick of the tongue. The known and loved particular child makes it possible for one to understand better and care more about all children.

It is far more clear to me now than when I came out of Mundugumor that a society that has ceased to care about children, a society that cuts off older people from meaningful contact with children, a society that segregates any group of men and women in such a way that they are prevented from having or caring for children, is greatly endangered. It seems to me that this is one reason why, today, in the Catholic missions in New Guinea, the faith of the priests and the lay brothers may falter, while the sisters, who care for little children and are close to them, can work on. It is extraordinarily difficult to love children in the abstract, to devote oneself exclusively to the next generation, or in speaking to actual children to tell them with conviction, "Boys and girls of America, you are the hope of the world"—as we were told by a speaker whose eyes ranged unseeing over the heads of my high-school class in 1917. It is only through precise, attentive knowledge of particular children that we can become—as we must—informed advocates for the needs of all children and passionate defenders of the right of the unconceived to be well born.

Early this year I spent a month living in my sister's hospitable home so that I could be a resource, but not a burden, in the nearby

Kassarjian household while Catherine and Barkev were preparing for a two-year work period in Iran. This crowded month, during which I could be a full-time grandmother to Vanni, has rounded out my understanding of something for which I have pleaded all my life—that everyone needs to have access both to grandparents and grandchildren in order to be a full human being.

In the presence of grandparent and grandchild, past and future merge in the present. Looking at a loved child, one cannot say, "We must sacrifice this generation for the next. Many must die now so that later others may live." This is the argument that generations of old men, cut off from children, have used in sending young men out to die in war. Nor can one say, "I want this child to live well no matter how we despoil the earth for later generations." For seeing a child as one's grandchild, one can visualize that same child as a grandparent, and with the eyes of another generation one can see other children, just as light-footed and vivid, as eager to learn and know and embrace the world, who must be taken into account—now. My friend Ralph Blum has defined the human unit of time as the space between a grandfather's memory of his own childhood and a grandson's knowledge of those memories as he heard about them. We speak a great deal about a human scale; we need also a human unit in which to think about time.

↵   ↵   ↵

Grandparenthood is, as Mead points out, an important life stage for many people. It can give life a renewed sense of generativity, and provide intimations of immortality.

Still a Son. Even when we become grandfathers, we may still be sons. Daughters become wives and mothers, but retain the role of daughter as long as a parent is alive. One of the predictable issues of aging is working out new relationships with our aging parents. There may be a long, relatively stable period of adult-adult relationships after children marry; relationships forged during this period may reflect antagonism, mutual support, or indifference.

As parents become very old and near death, new problems arise. Arrangements must be made for the ill parent who can no longer remain alone. Sometimes children assume financial responsibility for their old parents, although both parents and children resist this arrangement. Even if financial aid is not involved, the emotional strain and time demands may be considerable. One of the issues during this time is how to handle needs for assistance. The child grows up relying on the parent for help, and the parent role is partly defined in terms of help-giving. Adult parents and children work out patterns of reciprocal aid. During old age, the aid may become less reciprocal as the child becomes the giver and the parent the receiver. This, plus the frailty and loss of mental acuity that can accompany the predeath stages, challenges long-held conceptions of the parent-child relationship. Some speak of the changes in terms of role reversal, and many experience it with discomfort. Children do not wish to act as parents to an aging mother, and the mother may well wish she could retain her health and independence.

Such a situation may recreate conflicts and feelings associated with childhood. If the "child" does not figure out, as an adult, his new relationship to his parents, he may find himself unable to cope with his dying parents. We may treat our ailing parents as we feel our parents treated us. Parent-child relationships are inherently ambivalent, with admiration and gratitude coexisting alongside dismay and resentment. It would be beneficial for adults to learn to accept the complex nature of intimate human relationships, and not to be ruled by anger. They can acknowledge their wishes to be released from the burdens of caring for an ill, incontinent mother, without rejecting the mother herself.

A child learns to see the behavior of the parent as relevant to the parent's needs and limitations, and does not forever hold the parent responsible for real or imagined errors in child-rearing. However, emotionally immature adult children approach the deathbed of their parents with anxiety, realizing that they will not have time to work out a more satisfying relationship. Our parents' death signals our own mortality; it means that we are the eldest generation—and the next to go. The illness of a parent may arouse great anxiety because it increases our own sense of vulnerability.

6

friends and lovers: together and apart

> *Two are better than one, because they have a good reward for their toil. For if they fall, one will lift up his fellow; but woe to him who is alone when he falls and has not another to lift him up. Again, if two lie together, they are warm; but how can one be warm alone?* [1]

PARTNERS

Most Americans marry, at least once. The roles of husband and wife are highly significant to most adults; acquiring them has traditionally been seen as a transition into adulthood. As one ages, there are several likely changes in the spouse role. One may remain married to the same person whom one vowed to love "till death do you part." One may find marriage to the original partner more intolerable than the alternatives, and divorce. One may lose one's role involuntarily when one's husband or wife dies. One may find oneself single again, for a long or short time. And one may remarry and acquire a revised version of the spouse role. The uncertainties of the course of marriage are nicely captured in the words to a song done by the Beatles.

[1] *Ecclesiastes,* 4: 9–11.

When I'm Sixty-Four

John Lennon and Paul McCartney

When I get older, losing my hair,
Many years from now,
Will you still be sending me a Valentine,
Birthday greetings, bottle of wine?
If I'd been out 'till quarter to three
Would you lock the door?
Will you still need me, will you still feed me,
When I'm sixty-four?
You'll be older, too,
And if you say the word,
I could stay with you.
I could be handy, mending a fuse
When your lights have gone.
You can knit a sweater by the fireside,
Sunday morning go for a ride;
Doing the garden, digging the weeds,
Who could ask for more?
Will you still need me, will you still feed me,
When I'm sixty-four?
Every summer we can rent a cottage,
In the Isle of Wight, if it's not too dear;
We shall scrimp and save.
Grandchildren on your knee,
Vera, Chuck & Dave.
Send me a postcard, drop me a line,
Stating point of view;
Indicate precisely what you mean to say.
Yours sincerely, wasting away;
Give me your answer, fill in a form,
Mine for evermore.
Will you still need me, will you still feed me,
When I'm sixty-four?

The suitor above implies that he is not sure that romance and caring will survive into late maturity, even if the legal couple still exists. Most young people marry intending to remain together, but *we prepare people inadequately* for the inevitable changes that will occur in the relationship.

Carl Rogers, a psychologist of seventy-plus years and a half century of marriage, has written *Becoming Partners*,[2] a book which explores several marriages in depth. Rogers points out that marriage does not automatically create a partnership; it is an evolving process of becoming. From this own experience, his clinical practice, and special interviews with married couples, he has concluded that personal growth is one of the crucial ingredients in a successful marriage. Successful marriages are not placid and conflict-free; they tend to have times (not constant) of considerable conflict when both partners work out problems that impede their closeness. Out of crisis comes growth, if the crisis is handled adequately. Because the individuals in a marriage are likely to change as they grow older, change in the relationship is almost inevitable.

In addition, of course, the couple often must face certain unexpected situations: the birth of a defective child, the loss of a job, a property-destroying fire, a severe automobile accident, an invalid father moving into the household. The qualities of maturity, good sense, and intelligence needed to cope with such problems are not necessarily the ones which seem important during courtship.

Many studies have been done on marriage satisfaction over time, though most of the research suffers from a cross-sectional design that does not tell us how a particular marriage has changed. The more useful research conceptualizes marriage adjustment as a balance between negative and positive aspects. All marriages are gratifying in some respects and annoying in others for the participants.

To understand how marriage changes we must also remember that, as Jessie Bernard pointed out,[3] there are really *two* marriages in every partnership. There is ample evidence that husbands and wives experience and report marriage differently; they may differ on perceptions of frequency of sexual relations, amount of time spent together, division of household tasks, and even length of courtship; most couples

---

2 Carl Rogers. *Becoming Partners: Marriage and Its Alternatives.* (New York: Delacorte Press, 1972).

3 Jessie Bernard, *The Future of Marriage* (New York: World Publishing Company, 1972), p. 48.

do agree on the number of children they have! Research also indicates that marriage seems to be better for husbands than for wives, if we take measures of longevity, health, occupational success, criminality, happiness, and mental health. Bernard concludes that:

> It is wives who are driven mad, not by men but by the anachronistic way which marriage is structured today—or, rather, the life style which accompanies marriage today and which demands that all wives be housewives. In truth, being a housewife makes women sick.

Children affect the marriage relationship. Bernard summarizes the research on number of children: "Childless marriages tend to be happier than those with children, and small families tend to be happier than large ones." [4] Satisfaction with marriage seems more related to stage in the family cycle than to chronological age. Motherhood is generally more rewarding than is fatherhood, and the satisfaction with marriage over time reflects this.

Marriage satisfaction over the family life cycle was studied by Rollins and Feldman. [5] The prechild stage was the happiest, particularly for women. Wives' satisfaction fell to a low point with a teen-age child or young adult at home, and increased through the empty-nest period to a level approximating early marriage during the retirement years. Fathers showed a similar pattern, but greater satisfaction than wives at all the postchild periods; even adolescence was not as unsatisfactory to fathers as to mothers.

Further evidence of such a pattern in satisfaction over the history of parenthood was found by Lowenthal and her colleagues. Interviews with twenty-seven men and twenty-seven women approaching the "empty-nest" stage examined the impact on the marriage of children leaving home.

[4] *Ibid.*, p. 60.
[5] Boyd Rollins and Harold Feldman, "Marital Satisfaction Over The Family Life Cycle," *Journal of Marriage and the Family*, 32 (February, 1970), 20–28.

Transition to the Empty Nest: Marital Relationships

Marjorie Lowenthal and David Chiriboga

. . . Thus far, while we have reported some evidence for the existence of problems during the empty-nest period, with only a few exceptions, they do not seem to be of a nature to warrant use of the term crisis, and they rarely suggest that the pending departure of the youngest child is a cause of distress. There may be problems with that child, but they will be resolved (or overlooked) when he goes to college or gets his first job, or is no longer physically present on a day-to-day basis.

We now turn to an exploration of the thesis that the departure or pending departure of children may activate latent problems between spouses. In a section of the protocol devoted to perceptions of close others and of social networks, respondents were asked to describe their spouses, their agreements and disagreements, and their sexual attitudes and expectations. Perceptions of the spouse were grouped into two categories: positive or indulgently ambivalent, and negative. Consistent with their generally optimistic stance, the men spoke positively of their wives in a ratio of two to one, whereas women were twice as likely to describe their husbands in negative terms as to give positive appraisals. The majority of men described their wives in both expressive and instrumental terms, usually stressing their capacity for warmth and understanding, and then going on to discuss their competence as homemakers. Though more than half of these middle-aged men had wives who were working, their competencies or contributions in this area were not mentioned. Their few complaints about their wives had to do with extravagance or being too easygoing with the children. Women, on the other hand, tend to criticize their husbands for poor interpersonal relations, outside of the family, with the children, and, frequently, with themselves:

From "Transition to the Empty Nest," by Marjorie Fisk Lowenthal and David Chiriboga, in *Archives of General Psychiatry,* 26 (January 1972), pp. 12–13. © 1972 by the American Medical Association. Reproduced with permission of the authors and the American Medical Association.

He doesn't mix at all with people. He is not friendly . . . maybe it's shyness but I don't think so. He doesn't like people, period. He is . . . not a fighter. That annoys me sometimes. . . . If you want to argue, you just have to argue by yourself—he gets up and leaves.

We don't have fights, we are past that stage. That's the reason I live from day to day.

He is a master of passive resistance. He doesn't argue, he just keeps quiet. . . . He . . . can just turn people off.

Men and women were equally divided between those who said they have no disagreements or only mild ones and those who reported moderate-to-severe disagreements; and, not surprisingly, those whose descriptions of spouse were most critical were more likely to report severe disagreements. It should be added, however, that many wives volunteered the information that they do not have disagreements because they, the wives, placate their husbands. "I give in to him," as one put it; or "You have to learn to live with him and not do those things which upset him." While the most frequent area of disagreement between spouses had to do with child-rearing, there was no consistent pattern to these disagreements: men and women alike were as likely to believe that their spouses were too strict with the children as they were to consider them too permissive. The general tenor of these observations, however, was flat, without effect. They seem to be saying what is done is done, implying that once the last child has departed marital harmony will be restored:

. . . the main thing we really have our big arguments about is over our daughter. You know, because he feels that I'm taking her side too much, and more or less going against him. And I feel that I sort of want to protect her from him, because I think he gets too belligerent to her, instead of trying to talk sensibly; his temper gets away from him. . . . Because I don't want to be so strict that she'll feel she wants to run away from home or something. Whereas the way he acts toward her, it makes her want to feel that way. So I've got to be the sort of buffer in between. And that really gets his goats (sic), you know. . . . But then we keep telling each other, "Well, let's not get ourselves all upset over this." Because you know, we don't think she will be living at home all that much longer.

The generally more cheerful perspective of the men was further reflected in their reports on changes in sexual activity and satisfaction. The majority report that their sex life is about the same or better than it used to be. "We are freer now," says a 61-year-old carpenter, "it has

grown better from year to year." And a 48-year-old policeman elabo-
rated with a kind of lifecycle perspective:

> Oh yeah. When you are young, you're wild, just concerned with
> your own self-satisfaction. You don't know what it's all about but you
> think it's something that should be done. And most kids in their teens,
> it's just an accomplishment, a feat, something to brag about. But as you
> get older, you realize there's more to it. It's something not to be abused.
> It should occur at a happy time.

The majority of women, on the other hand, report a decline in
frequency or quality or both. For many, however, this does not so much
represent a disappointing change as a relief. One woman reports a
complete cessation of sex life and goes on to say, "I'm happy about it.
I am not a sexy person and I never have been." Others are content with
a decline:

> It's probably dwindled. Probably more on my part. I never got
> much out of sex personally.

> I don't have as much interest as I used to. . . . You have so many
> things to do you don't have the time . . . the desire is still there but
> it's just not so often. Jack is nice and sometimes he does things that are
> just as good as sex relations.

While at first glance this difference in attitude might be interpreted as a reflection of menopausal problems in women, we find little
support for such a thesis in these data. None reported severe menopausal problems, only four reported moderate ones, and the rest only
mild difficulties or none at all. . . . They are very matter-of-fact if not
offhand about the matter, several of them expressing gratitude for the
advances of modern medicine.   ↜

↜ ↜ ↜

Thus, you can expect that even if you remain married to the same
person for many years, the relationship will change. You and your
partner will both change as individuals, and your world will change.
You could develop one of the newest and potentially most exciting
kinds of marriage—the "mature marriage." In 1900, one partner (usually the husband) typically died before the last child left home. Now,
the average couple can count on fourteen to sixteen years of married
life together after the children are on their own.

You may wake up one morning and stare across the table at your mate, wondering where all the children went and what happened to that young person you married. You may "rediscover" each other, and find that your increased maturity, leisure, and financial resources enable you to forge a new and even more rewarding partnership for the second twenty-five years. This is a definite possibility—for those who manage to grow individually and still remain friends and lovers.

You may, however, stare at the person who has shared your bed for several decades, and find an unwelcome stranger.

BECOMING SEPARATE

The divorce statistics make it quite clear that not all marriages survive the parenting years to become more satisfying in later maturity. During the middle years, with the empty nest, career evaluation, internal personality changes, and signs of advancing physical age, many marriages are in a period of turmoil. Several authors analyzing problems of middle-aged men warn wives to be sympathetic and understanding and not to agree if the previously loving husband asks for a divorce. Middle age, for many men, is comparable to adolescence, with questions about self-identity, renewed concern with sexual performance, and a revival of power struggles—this time in terms of handling middle-aged power wisely and resisting attempts of young men to wrest it from them. The marriage arena may seem a safer place to "solve" these problems; a man might not be able to get another comparable job, but there seem to be plenty of available women.

Middle age is a critical period for marriage, and the outcome of the reevaluation may be either renewed vigor and satisfaction, resignation, or a definite lowered satisfaction. Many, but not all, of persons experiencing the latter become divorced. The process is invariably painful. An interesting autobiographical account of a period of separation which resolved into reinvolvement is in *Separation: Journal of a Marriage* by Eve Baguedor.[6] The process of divorce in middle age is analyzed by Mackey Brown below, as she considers what she and her husband might have done to save their marriage. It is wise to note that we have "her" marriage presented; as Ms. Brown realizes, "his" perspective would be different.

[6] Eve Baguedor, *Separation: Journal of a Marriage* (New York: Simon and Schuster, 1972).

Keeping Marriage Alive Through Middle Age

Mackey Brown

Something malignant is happening to middle-age marriage. All over the country, in cities and suburbs and small towns alike, couples in their middle years are breaking up. Not only do the divorces of the great and the near-great decorate the headlines; our solid old friends, whose 20- and 30-year marriages we took for granted, turn up every day in the cold statistics. Why do they fail, these marriages whose roots were sturdy enough to nourish a relationship for that long? Are there any answers, alternatives to divorce, that might have been found—in time? These questions urgently concern me today, for I am one of those statistics. I live with George Meredith's words roiling the surface of my mind: "No morning can restore what we have forfeited." And yet, and yet—I do believe the utter finality of divorce can be avoided if one moves with knowledge and foresight in time. On the eve of our thirty-first wedding anniversary, my husband and I at last acknowledged that we were facing a moribund/marriage. We had known, subconsciously at least, that we had been simply hanging on, white-knuckled: but hating the absolute dichotomy that society lays upon us—divorce or desperation, love it or leave it—we had put off the dissolution as long as possible. Finally the possible became impossible; we put ourselves in the practiced hands of the law, which disposed of our 31 years with great dispatch.

It was an "amicable" divorce. We still see each other frequently, looking back, not with those saddest words, "it might have been," but more in Willa Cather's sense that "the end is nothing, the road is all." And now that the necessity for self-justification has lessened, we can wonder together why we could not have foreseen the pressures of middle age, why we allowed bad habits to groove themselves so deeply into our lives that we could not find a way to erase them.

We had had a good marriage, falling in love not just out of

"Keeping Marriage Alive," by Mackey Brown © 1973 by Mackey Brown. Originally appeared in *McCall's*, January, 1973. Used by permission of the author.

infatuation, but for such reasons as respect, tenderness, shared humor, sexual attraction—even innocence. But these qualities were swiftly swallowed up in the necessities of living. A man may not choose a woman for her child-rearing abilities, her dishwashing skills, or floor-scrubbing techniques, but these can often overwhelm or diminish the more vital values.

We married poor and worked up from tiny apartments with orange-crate furniture to what today is called "security." With no differences in race, religion or how we saw the world, we had little to discover about each other; we simply marched, in lockstep, like creatures on their way to Noah's Ark.

We had the requisite two children and wove our lives about them. And marked as our generation was by the Great Depression, or goaded by the Puritan ethic, we used up the years making sure the kids' lives would be secure, secure, secure.

In doing so, we neglected to notice each other except as partners in a project. I did not see until lately that the quality he most loved in me—of wonder, a quick and eager curiosity—had been lost in the demands on any wife for instant certainties, judgments: "Don't you dare run across that busy street. . . . No, we can't afford it. . . . Not now, I'm busy." What I most loved in him—a capacity for seeing into the heart of many matters—became corrupted by success, became dogmatic, authoritarian. Humor and tenderness turned into luxuries too heavy to carry in our race to that undefined finish line.

We never sneaked small vacations away from the children; sex became a bedroom ritual, almost meaningless except as a tension reliever. We never even went out for a quiet dinner alone, to say "Who are you, and how are you?"—at first we had no money, and later we were too caught up in everyday sociality. Our conversation seldom touched on life, liberty or important things; we talked of new bathroom fixtures and where to find money for college for the kids.

Finally we hit our late 40s, when the money crunch eased and job security became less of an electric cattle prod. But by then the children had grow up and said with some heat (as they should have) that they no longer wanted our hovering concern. They moved out, and with them went the notion of Family. We were left to stare astonished across the breakfast table, strangers in a stranger land.

At first, our parting seemed inevitable. Looking back, I think not. We were indeed strangers. But if we had had courage enough to push aside the waste and wear of those savage getting-and-spending days, we could have helped each other rediscover the old beloved qualities.

I remember last year, when my husband met me at an airport, feeling a familiar surge of denial when I saw him: "That's not Walter, not my tall, gangling bridegroom with that endearing openness. Who is this heavy, knowing man with florid face and half-white hair?" Disbelief flashed across his face, too, when he caught sight of me, my one-time wonderment hidden behind glittering glasses, the old perception replaced by anxiety lines stitched into my face. They were momentary twinges, perhaps, but reminders that we do not see the change; we only behold the changed—often with anger instead of understanding.

We knew, of course, about the empty-nest syndrome but were not perceptive enough to recognize it in ourselves. It did not occur to us that to grow gracefully into a new kind of life required an affectionate search for the neglected, unused parts of ourselves. Instead, we supinely accepted the dictum of our youth-oriented society: that to be our age was to be defeated.

In our fear at what we saw in ourselves and in the middle-aged casualties around us, we began to latch onto each other, tighter and tighter, feeding on each other like ghouls. My husband took out his most familiar too, logic: He would teach me how to be. He hectored me about how uselessly I spent my days, fuming when he came home at night and found me watching the television news. He found my friends inconsequential, my lovemaking unimaginative, my life-style unproductive—and said so, day after day after day.

I can't say he was wrong in his judgments, but in the old days his ability to see inside people was tempered with concern for their growth. Now the constant belittling turned me into a knotted skein of emotional snarls: the more he twitched at my loose ends, the tighter the knots became. What he thought of as constructive criticism felt, piled on my back, like a growing stack of last straws. I retreated into periodic depressions, sitting around in sullen silence—or, when I could no longer contain my anger, nagging, picking, complaining of his drinking, making snide remarks about his teaching, jealously demanding to know since he found me so incompetent, whether he had had found someone better.

We must have used most of the weapons in the marital arsenal —all the irritating gestures, hard eyes, slammed doors, the dramatic rush to the tranquilizer bottle, a certain way of prinking the mouth.

What we thought of as slashing sarcasm (I, watching him pour himself a heavy drink, "Can you get it all in one glass, dear?," or he, walking past me at the makeup mirror, "Now there's a study in futility") produced furies that reverberated like ripples on a lake before a storm.

All was not conflict in our barren universe, of course; sometimes life became merely dreary. There were periods of determined "getting along together," with little rushes of conversation, some attempts to break through the myths of menopause, male and female, that lie heavy over a sagging sex life—followed by intervals of cold neglect.

We might have tried counseling at that point, but even now it seems to me that marriage counselors are hung up on compromise— stuffing grudges into gunnysacks, resentments into some closet of the mind. Compromise demands acceptance of the other's flaws rather than searching for latent growth in oneself—and at 50 one should not be concerned with who is using whom but with how to use onself. Couples who keep pressing on, trying to contain each other, can only fail: The law in middle-aged marriage is that possession is nine-tenths of the *loss*. What is needed is more and more laissez faire.

But my husband and I were not bright enough to say let it be. Although we desperately needed a margin in which to find ourselves, we were jammed into each other's pockets by the mores of marriage— not out of affection but because custom dictates that couples be seen everywhere together like pairs of mating birds. I should have taken myself by the scruff of my neck and gone off somewhere alone, to get my head together, to find my own compass again, instead of living by rituals and reactions that were learned on the line of family action.

In their late 40s and early 50s, people suffer a sort of second adolescence, surging about in a sea of hormonal changes, fearful of the intimations of mortality they feel as they read the obituary columns. Inwardly they sense that if they do not achieve some kind of growth for the second period of their lives, they will have "Died at Fifty, Buried at Seventy-Five" engraved on their tombstones.

But like all too many middle-aged couples today, we made no move to loosen the bonds of conjugality; we simply sat still with our resentment. Tiny things took on a ridiculous intensity. A scowl above a newspaper, the creak of the liquor-cabinet door, a nervous out-of-time humming, a "Where have you been?"—all became push buttons with programmed responses. (My mother used to wash out her throat each morning with a particularly atrocious sound; it is the only thing my father ever mentioned about her, even long after their divorce.)

Physical separation can relieve some of that emotional tension. Where there is money enough even to consider divorce, I believe that money would be better spent on trips—alone—for weekends or longer. I know a wife without money who sometimes house-sits for people in our town, people who need their canary fed or their house-plants watered. Her husband shows up to take her out to dinner, often staying the night with her in a delightful illusion of illicit sex—with a strange woman in a strange bed.

But physical separation is only a prelude to the more urgent need: mental disengagement—learning to live with the words, No Trespass. I know now that the way to find Thoreau's "inward morning" of the second half of life is to shift the focus of thinking away from one's mate and onto oneself. I had been trying to find answers in terms of Walter's behavior ("If you'll stop drinking, I'll stop nagging you about it"); I couldn't see my own cheap rationalizations for what they were ("I can't help it, that's just the way I am"). A clue to this came during the period between the filing of our divorce and the final papers, when our sex life took on an exciting renaissance: No longer inhibited by worry over what the other was doing or feeling, we simply took what came and enjoyed it. But we ignored the clue: By that time we were each so caught up in our own self-righteousness and martyrdom—what he had done to me! how I had disappointed him!—that we did not explore this new dimension.

I am learning now, with the help of such books as Eric Berne's *Games People Play* and *I'm OK—You're OK,* by Thomas A. Harris, to uncover some of the whys of my own behavior. What was the basis for my insecurity? Did I nag out of a misplaced power drive? Why did I flinch so at his philandering? Could I not have seen that our kind of too-heavy twosomeness would drive any man to other companionship, especially the comfort of someone who does not know (as a wife knows and cannot *un*know) what he has done or left undone?

Self-discovery can be devastating, but down among the ugly fissures of fact lie the outcroppings of the unused self many of us ignored during the violent years of "making it" for the family. I look now for traces of the small talent for writing I once had—can I mine it now in this second period of my life? The idea is exhilarating.

Paul Douglas in his book, *In the Fullness of Time,* says the old have more going for them than is normally assumed. New growth, new directions lie open for those willing to suffer the growing pains of a second adolescence. Some might feel a little silly going back to college among the young, but I have a friend who just got a degree in counseling at 49; from a rather vacant and hypochondriacal person, she has become confident and excited about the future. Another went into politics, via the League of Women Voters, earning her husband's admiration—and giving him time to write. A man friend of mine, tired of a job he had already milked of whatever satisfaction it could give him, has redirected his aptitude for Saturday-night gambling and become a serious and successful student of the stock market.

Merely distracting hobbies can be made creative by figuring out how to make them relate to the world: in Simone de Beauvoir's phrase, "pursuing ends that give our existence meaning." A middle-aged friend whose cooking talents were wasted on her dieting husband now takes her exotic goodies to a retirement home where the people are tired of institutional food. Another's love of nature led her to work out wilderness pack trips geared to the age and abilities of other middle-lifers. A botany professor, alarmed at the ecological damage he saw, has made himself an expert on pollution control.

Growth does not necessarily involve carving out whole new careers. Sometimes the simple satisfying of a lifelong dream can symbolize a new thrust toward life. A couple of years ago, my husband bought a pantherish little sports car he could not really afford. I should have recognized the flamboyance for what it was: the fulfillment of a dream from as far back as when he learned to steer a car standing between his father's knees. But caught up in my own compulsions and suspicions, I saw that car only as an image-maker—the fast-driving, aggressive, sexual male decked out to attract little college cuties. I destroyed his pleasure with taunts and sneers, instead of allowing him to propel himself through it into a rebirth of joy in living.

Women, too, have unquenchable dreams—oddly enough, of romance. In middle life especially, despite sagging breasts and quilted thighs, they yearn for small touches of tenderness, an invitation to take a hand-in-hand walk under the stars, or sentimental references to things they were once beloved for. I think few fiftyish husbands realize how poignant such signs are to their wives, how consequential they can be in helping women to regenerate in themselves the qualities that once made them desirable.

But regardless of how much it means to have understanding from one's mate, the search for a new self is still a solitary one and should not be dependent upon anyone else. Living alone now, without my old preoccupation with my husband's world, I find solitude soothing. My sense of wonder renews itself every day: I walk in fields of wild flowers, touching one, really seeing it. I reread old books with joy, books that were simply print on a page during the years when I read with one eye on the clock and the other on the stove. I look forward to the cocktail hour—with friends or with my ex-husband—without the nervous apprehension that it will signal an unloading of the day's grievances. My mind is smoothing out; even my face is losing its tension lines, as the acid of anger leaches out of me. But I miss my marriage. I miss its continuity and companionship. I wish I could have learned earlier what I am learning now.

For I believe that middle-aged marriage, lived as it should be and can be, offers qualities that nothing else has ever superseded: A shelter where two people can grow older without loneliness, the ease of long intimacy, family jokes that don't have to be explained, understanding without words. Most of all it offers memories. The inexpressible sweetness of first love, a warm back in a wide bed, a child in a basket wearing its first smile, a sudden, shared surge of pride at a kid on a stage, a moment looking up at each other across a chessboard. Can these memories, having been shared, ever be replaced?

This is a rather simplistic analysis of one marriage; others have different difficulties. But I suspect that the underlying causes of middle-aged divorce remain roughly the same. No magic can transmute a sour marriage; the fairies will not simply take it away. Thoreau says, "To regret deeply is to live afresh," but surely it would be better to use one's imagination to seek alternatives, solutions—to live afresh before it is too late. Drifting into divorce may be one alternative to living in quiet desperation, but without doubt it is the least affirmative of them all.

"TILL DEATH DO US PART"

The loss of the husband or wife role may not come through divorce but with death. Women, particularly, can anticipate widowhood—

particularly if they marry men older than themselves. There is some evidence that women anticipate widowhood and begin to prepare for it; there are indications, too, that young women today will be much better prepared for widowhood (and divorce) than are their mothers and grandmothers.

One of the more systematic studies of widowhood among urban American women over fifty was supervised by Helena Lopata.[7] She makes the excellent point that current studies of widowhood reflect the experiences of people "brought up under conditions not likely to be duplicated in future generations of human beings." However, we can learn from the past and present how to arrange for our future.

Lopata found three patterns of adjustment in her sample of widows. Most widows went through an initial period of grief and disorientation; even if the spouse's death is a lingering one, the end means role-loss and finality. The ways in which the women re-engaged in society reflected their long-term patterns of activity. One group of "modern" women had a history of involvement in many activities, evidence of problem-solving abilities, and flexibility in social roles. Such a woman is able to re-examine her own life-styles and goals when she loses her husband and reorient her activities into personally gratifying areas. I have known women who "bloomed" after widowhood; freed from many of the responsibilities of housekeeping and serving a husband, they direct energies into paid or volunteer work and demonstrate great competence.

Lopata also found some widows who lived in ethnic communities, psychologically separate from the city as a whole. Being immersed in kin relations, a very close peer group, or a network of neighbors, such a woman may continue many of her involvements with little modification after becoming a widow. This is particularly true of the lower-class urbanite. A similar lack of change may apply in the case of a suburbanite who had never developed multifaceted relations with the husband, but lived in a sex-segregated world.

Some widows meet the stereotype of social isolation. Such women have often been passive all their adult lives, and have not learned to establish independent interests and contacts outside their small circle of friends. If contact with these friends are lost, because of health, death, or poor finances, she lacks the ability to make new friends.

Men who are widowed face many of the same problems of loss

[7] Helena Lopata, *Widowhood in An American City* (Schenkman Publishing Co., 1973, distributed by General Learning Press, Morristown, N.J.).

faced by the widow. In addition, they may find it difficult to cope on a day-to-day basis. While women are used to caring for themselves and others, men may be used to being cared for. The domestic routines and responsibilities which accompany widowerhood can be devasting. Men who have, during their married life, become competent in self-care and domestic responsibilities (e.g., shopping, cooking, laundry, keeping one's own environment relatively well-organized and clean, etc.) are not so dependent and helpless when widowed.

What factors make for good adjustment in widowhood? If we wish to plan ahead, what should we emphasize? The answers are related, of course, to general issues of coping successfully with aging, which we shall discuss more fully in Chapter 11. Here, we should examine the evidence on readjustment to single state in later life.

SWINGING OR SOLITARY?

Both divorce and widowhood represent the loss of a significant social role and the shift into a less well defined one. The nonmarried role is usually associated with adolescence and young adulthood, or with advanced old age. The young single role has fairly clear expectations for behavior; dating and mating are considered important, with the anticipation of settling into a long-term marriage commitment.

The middle-aged or older adult who becomes single again enters an uncertain situation. Shared norms may be developing among the formerly married,[8] but the expected behavior is often not clear until the person actually becomes single. Perhaps there is more consensus on appropriate behavior for widowed than divorced people. There are also important psychological differences: widowhood, particularly in later life, represents the "natural" end of a relationship. While there may be regret over certain aspects of the marriage, it endured to fulfill the marriage vows. Divorce is not an anticipated end of marriage, and it may involve more guilt and hopes of a second marriage that would more adequately meet the felt needs.

Those of us who become single again as older adults will face certain predictable problems, regardless of whether divorce or death was the cause. The first problem is often that of maintaining a similar, satisfying standard of living, since most couples manage better finan-

[8] See Morton Hunt, *The World of the Formerly Married* (New York: McGraw-Hill, 1966).

cially than do single persons—this is particularly true if both partners earn money. Divorced men and women often find it very expensive to maintain two households; if the husband assumes the responsibility of maintaining his former wife (few do), he will have few resources left for "swinging," let alone supporting a second family. A singled man must pay for his housekeeping services, do them himself, or do without. The result of any of these options is a reduced standard of living, particularly when men are not experienced in efficient household management.

Divorced and widowed women without an independent source of income often find themselves with a greatly reduced financial status; this limits their participation in social life and accounts for much of their unhappiness. Divorcees have the additional problems of continued hassles over money awarded as alimony or child support; money can provide a continuing tie to an otherwise discarded relationship. The problems of a singled, middle-aged wife can be acute if she has no independent life and income, as many women do not. They may find that they are, as Johnie Tillman has observed, one man away from welfare.

Financial difficulties relate to another problem: reinvolvement in society. Many widows and widowers withdraw somewhat from their usual social involvements during the period preceding and following death or divorce; when they emerge, they may find their former patterns impossible to maintain. A divorced couple find it difficult to remain friends with the people they knew as a couple; this may become less of a problem as divorce becomes more common. However, the search for a new identity and a new partner often must be carried out among new acquaintances. Making new friends as an individual is not easy for many older people, particularly when their single status raises issues of possible romance, dating, and mating. Dating is an adolescent activity in our culture, and it is difficult to know how to behave as a middle-aged, formerly married date.

Many do not wish to resume serious courtship right away, and some may not seek remarriage. They would enjoy companionship, but how should that be achieved? Can they interest someone besides the former mate? Can they be interested? Can they build a new relationship, unwilling as they are in middle age to make the kinds of compromises they might have made in youth? What about sex?

After experiencing sex with a legal, readily available partner for many years, the singled may feel acutely deprived sexually. Obviously, an elderly widowed woman who believed sexual life ceased with the menopause will not be troubled by this particular loss. Many middle-aged and older persons are troubled; for the widowed, particularly, this is usually not an issue openly acknowledged. When the singled reestablishes social ties and begins dating, the matter of sexual activity invariably arises. We can expect this to become more of an issue as we accept sexuality as belonging to men and women throughout the life cycle.

Hunt, in his book on the formerly married, describes the "natural course" of sexual affairs, and sees them as important ways to learn about oneself. Divorced people, at least, seem to go through a period of promiscuous behavior. However, sex without emotional attachment is not very satisfying for most adults, particularly if they have ever experienced a committed shared sexuality.

The extent of sexual deprivation depends on the availability of partners. Older women may suffer from stereotypes of sexual desirability and may find few men who are willing and able to be satisfactory lovers. Under a traditional double standard of sexual behavior, women were assumed to trade sex for the desired romance and security, and men to trade romance and security for the sex they wanted. While this may or may not be an accurate reflection of the current older generation, it seems even less true of the younger generation. As attitudes about sexuality change, so will the experience of being singled in middle age or in later maturity. If men and women in their youth learn to value and expect mutuality of committed caring concern in their sexual behavior, or if they learn to enjoy casual, uncommitted sexual relations, these attitudes will be important in their reaction to being singled.

Lopata suggested four processes important to adjustment in widowhood;[9] they seem equally helpful in facilitating adjustment to the death of a marriage by divorce. The processes include:

1) **Grief Work:** When we have suffered a great loss, we need to mourn the loss, to talk about it, to acknowledge the loss to ourselves and others. Our society seems ambivalent about loss; it often makes us uncomfortable to hear of a death or a divorce; we wonder if our loss may be next. However, it is important to grieve and come to terms with the meaning of the loss. The resolute widower who never sheds a tear, even in private, is not prepared to put his life together again.

[9] *Op. cit.*, 271–277.

2) **Companionship:** When one spouse is removed from the household, the remaining person must learn to live alone. Divorced people may celebrate the legal decree with a grand party, but there are many hours during the process of becoming divorced and after the party when the person is alone and might appreciate even passive companionship. A one-person household means there is no one around whom to schedule the day and share routine events. Singled women, especially, often feel unwanted in social situations; they may want to accept social invitations but do not want to be pitied. They may be ignored because it is difficult for friends to know how to cope with issues of death and divorce. There may be jealousy, married women fearing that a singled woman will be available for their husbands.

3) **Problem Solving and Building Competence:** Singled people need to learn to solve their own problems in ways that are personally satisfying. As Lopata found, widows are often beset with well-meaning advice from friends, relatives, and lawyers; if they take it they may make decisions they later regret. They also perpetuate their self-image of helplessness and dependence, which is likely to be a real problem, particularly since these signify old age for many. Individuals who have gone through a divorce often have had their sense of competence challenged, and they, too, need to establish ways of coping with their problem. Friends can be helpful to the widowed or divorced, e.g., in making funeral arrangements, loaning money, and helping solve other immediate problems, but they should refrain from urging any major changes in life-style.[10]

4) **Help in Re-Engagement:** Lopata discusses some of the community services which help a widow become reinvolved, such as widow-to-widow visiting. Hunt talks of the "invisible underground" of formerly married people who help introduce singled adults to the social circuit when they are ready. There are some formal organizations specifically for singled persons, and a very few for older (over thirty-five or forty singled. It seems that an important part of the re-engagement process should be some therapeutic relationships which would help the individual deal with the past and prepare for the future. Alternatives should be explored, particularly since the options open to older singleds may not be clear. There are usually more choices to make than the individual realizes. The choices include re-engagement—and marriage.

10 These specific suggestions, and many others, are included in Lopata's book on widowhood.

THE SECOND HONEYMOON

When the singled person has survived the mourning and adjustment periods, there are usually strong urges to regain a satisfying life-style. The patterns this may take will probably depend largely on the social status and biopsychological age of the individual.

There are virtually no systematic studies of mating and dating patterns in middle and old age, and it is difficult to assess how much of the apparent change in norms and activity exists in the popular press and how much in the private lives of many. The young are more open about their behavior, and probably begin their sexual activity earlier. But they seem, if anything, more in favor of sex only within a mutually caring, responsible relationship. If such ideals are carried into later life they may contribute to increased divorce rates; if both partners are not satisfied, they may not "stick it out" through old age. Their mating patterns after divorce would not be likely to result in legal marriage commitments, but rather in a series of personally meaningful relationships.

It is possible that we can anticipate a sizable minority of older adults exhibiting a life-style resembling a less energetic version of that of the middle-class young adult today. Such a life-style would resolve some problems currently experienced by older adults, but would surely create new ones.

There seem to be basic human tendencies operating to make marriage attractive. As Jessie Bernard points out,[11] humans basically want two contradictory things: stability and variety. For this reason, marriage as now conceptualized is bound to create difficulties in not providing sufficient variety for some people. However, the need for continuity is best met within marriage; as Mackey Brown wrote, no new partner can ever share earlier memories. Also, perpetually creating new alliances takes energy. For many reasons, many older singled persons seek to establish a new marriage.

Most men with reasonable health and economic resources remarry within a few years, usually to a younger woman. Middle-aged women may remarry, particularly if they have retained a youthful ap-

11 Jessie Bernard, *The Future of Marriage* (New York: World Publishing Co., 1972).

pearance, although women at all ages remain attractive to at least some men.

Remarriage means the acquisition of many new social roles. The spouse role is regained, and most of the norms are similar to those for a first marriage. However, the first marriage is always part of the second; it is common knowledge among those who have tried it that the second wife marries the first family, not just the husband. The second wife will probably acquire new roles, as stepmother or stepgrandmother; she may also acquire new in-laws. The older the couple are at remarriage, the less likely it is that they will have problems with relatives. Middle-aged remarriages may have difficulties in managing the complex arrangements and feelings involved in meshing a potential three families (his, hers, and their new one). Arguments over money and comparisons with the former spouse are almost inevitable. Given the evidence that teen-age and young-adult children create strains for any marriage, it is no surprise if remarriages during this period have a rough honeymoon.

Problems encountered often revolve around financial arrangements, particularly if one partner brings substantially more to the marriage than does the other. Possessions of a lifetime maintain continuity with the past; this may be reassuring to the owner, but disconcerting to the new spouse. More successful resolutions include a new household with some favored possessions of each, and some new joint possessions—particularly a bed of their own.

Children can cause problems for older parents wishing to remarry after a divorce or death. Parents with money may have children who look forward to inheriting the wealth and the possessions, and who resent an "'intruder" taking their heritage. The children may also resent the implication that someone else could "replace" their parent, and they may feel uneasy at a reminder of sexual interests of their older parent. However, children may also welcome the remarriage of their parent, recognizing the continued needs for intimacy and companionship—and/or being relieved at having someone else to care for the parent.

But remarriage in the postparental period can be very successful.[12] The most successful second marriages in later maturity seem to be those where the partners have known each other for many years.

[12] Walter McKain, *Retirement Marriage* (Storrs, Conn: Storrs Agricultural Experiment Station Monograph 3, 1969).

Often after death has taken two spouses, the survivors in a circle of friends will marry. Such alliances have many advantages; the couple can preserve much continuity and can build a life together on a shared past. Friends can remain the same, and they may share fond memories of former mates. Most important, they are likely to be familiar with each other's peculiarities and basic values, and they are able to assess realistically whether hey can live together successfully.

Unsuccessful remarriages among older adults probably share many flaws of other unhappy unions. Basic personality problems that are not dealt with directly will seldom be resolved in a second marriage. Older adults who have a brief courtship with a previously unknown person are unlikely to establish a durable marriage; this is probably even more true for them than for young adults, because they have experienced at least one marriage already and have formed habits and expectations.

People get together, and drift apart, throughout adulthood. Relationships change as people and circumstances change. Humans continue to work out patterns to meet fundamental needs for closeness. Friends are important throughout life. Anticipating that friends (and lovers) will be lost as we grow older, we need to maintain friendship skills. These skills may be learned at any age, and they must be used to develop new friendships and to nurture our current ones. Making friends involves some risk; we need to be able to take the risks and reap the rewards.

7

work and leisure:
jet plane or rocking chair?

> *Then I looked on all the works that my hands had wrought, and on the labor that I had labored to do; and behold, all was vanity and vexation of spirit, and there was no profit under the sun.*[1]

What good is work? What does your work provide you with—money for the grocer and books? An obligation to be somewhere at certain times of the week? Feelings of competence when things go well, and vexation when you make serious errors? How would your life be different if you had no work?

The meanings of work change for all of us over the course of our lives; probably your view of work has already changed considerably from your childhood years when you had fantasies of being an airplane pilot, a cowboy, a ballerina, or a teacher. You may have started working at home with small chores, done paid work part time during school, and then worked full time. In our society, you can look forward to retirement from full-time paid work in your sixties; some predict this will be lowered to the fifties. You can plan for a healthy period of your life to indulge in—what? The "what" is the challenge of the retirement years.

The challenge facing all of us is to plan our adult years to end up with (1) financial security rather than a marginal existence or pov-

[1] *Ecclesiastes* 2:11

erty; and (2) activities that we find interesting and pleasurable rather than hours of nothingness or "make work."

WORK AND SOCIETY

The Protestant ethic was a foundation of our country; the measure of a man was his work productivity, and occupational success indicated God's favor. It was a system under which individual effort was to be rewarded, and the poor were poor because they lacked merit. Thus, continued work was extremely important into old age; the individual must provide for himself. The Depression of the thirties did much to alter that belief: it became obvious that external events could overwhelm multitudes of hard-working individuals. Social remedies had to be found for social problems, and the Social Security Act was passed to give federal financial support to aged and dependent persons. Since aging benefits could be received at sixty-five, that age has become a significant one. Many view it as signaling the onset of a new stage in life, centered on retirement from work and increased leisure.

Retirement from work serves a useful social function in an era when labor supply exceeds demand. Retirement removes people from the work force and opens jobs for younger people; it allows promotions of middle-aged people into responsible positions; and it eliminates the need to retain workers whose knowledge and skills may be outdated. Like the period of adolescence, unknown in earlier, less technologically advanced, cultures, that of retirement is a relatively recent phenomenon. In fact, the time devoted to work has decreased greatly over the decades, and we can expect the decrease to continue. Four-day weeks will be common for many workers, the working day itself may shorten, and normal retirement may come in the fifties. These social changes already have a profound impact on the personal experience of retirement.

SEX, SOCIAL CLASS, AND WORK

People in different social classes look at retirement differently. Also, men and women have traditionally had different work experiences. The differences in work experience over a lifetime means that the experience of retirement from work will not be the same for all.

Working-class men and women begin paid work early in life; women who work at home often resume paid jobs on a regular or sporadic basis for financial reasons. Work provides money for survival and for satisfying activities, and it is a source of friends. Men's jobs are not necessarily poorly paid, but inflation makes it difficult to save for old age. Many men report little intrinsic job satisfaction, and they welcome retirement; most would retire earlier than sixty-five if they had enough money. Working-class women typically have poor jobs, particularly if they are not unionized. They have little training, and many would prefer full-time homemaking, at least during child-rearing years. Most studies of older working-class women indicate they welcome retirement with relief. The sense of identity and satisfaction may come partly from work for working-class men and women, but increasingly it seems to come from involvement in family and leisure-time activities Thus, for such persons the primary problem with retirement is financial.

Middle-class men have traditionally been firm believers in the Protestant ethic and oriented to work for a sense of identity and achievement. Young men set out to build careers, and they establish personal goals and often personal timetables. Middle age brings increased career complexity and responsibility.

Bernice Neugarten supervised research on 100 men and women, aged 30 to 60, who were highly successful occupationally. The following comments draw from unpublished materials made available by Dr. Neugarten, as well as from her published research papers. Five major issues emerged in terms of careers in the Neugarten sample; these issues are also themes in other discussions of middle-class careers.

(1) A sense of **increased complexity and responsibility** was felt by many of the respondents. They had more individual responsibility: the buck stopped with them. Some thrived on this, and got pleasure from the sense of mastery. Others felt it to be a burden, and tried to delegate more responsibility. Presumably there would be more individuals with this reaction in a group of moderately successful men and women. In addition to responsibility, time pressures were common. Time becomes precious in middle age, and these individuals struggled with multiple demands; some felt that the job was running them. Many were unused to the idea of leisure or recreation. A third aspect of the increased complexity is dealing with technological change. In fields where knowledge and technique expand rapidly, the middle-aged individual who has moved out of technical and into management posi-

tions may feel threatened by younger men, and "out of date." The high achievers balanced this by emphasizing the importance of understanding the broader perspective.

(2) The middle-aged high achiever also has to deal with issues involving **interpersonal relationships.** Some were irritated by ambitious young coworkers; the more mature emphasized using their interpersonal skills to soothe things over, while the more threatened were less tolerant with the young. The middle-agers included "peers" of a broader range of ages than earlier in their lives. Perhaps the most delicate issue is that of psychological distancing, maintaining cordial but noninvolved relationships with subordinates. This issue is reflected in the remark to me by a professor: "When you become a department chairman, you lose your friends." This man recognized that his new position of authority meant that he could not risk having favoritism interefere with the smooth functioning of the department.

(3) The department chairman quoted above reflects the third major theme in mid-life careers: **maintaining power, authority, and autonomy.** Lack of control over one's career situation is seen as evidence of failure. The middle-aged careerist is concerned with strategies to keep his success and power increasing, or at least to keep it from declining. Some exploit the privileges of rank to the utmost to keep, at least, the appearance of success. Status can be enhanced by windows, carpets, two secretaries, and some assistants. A special concern of middle age in terms of maintaining power is in figuring out how to select, train, and give appropriate responsibility to the people who can carry on one's work.

(4) **Career review** is a common phenomenon at mid-life. The high achievers in Neugarten's study were articulate in describing the process. On the basis of evaluating past, present, and anticipated future success, a fairly stable career identity is established. The sense of limited time left may produce anxiety in individuals who have not reached the peak of their career and who worry that they may not.

Saunders[2] is one of the many writers who have discussed mid-life discontent with work. He outlines the typical problem situation of executives: men in their late forties bucking for top management and realizing that most won't make it. They feel trapped; quite successful men may dream of escaping the boredom and lack of challenge on the job, preferably with a second career. However, relatively few actually

2 Dero A. Saunders, "Executive Discontent" in *Man, Work and Society,* S. Nosow and W. H. Form, editors (New York: Basic Books, 1962), pp. 461–67.

change careers; the job market does not welcome fifty-year-old men, and there are few training programs available for middle-age men. Saunders reported that most executives decided the investment in their current job skills overweighed the risks of mastering a new field. Neugarten found very similar feelings among the 100 high achievers, lending support to this as a "normal" career issue at middle age.

(5) The process of **retirement** begins in middle age with the awareness that time left is limited. Often career re-evaluation is related to anticipated retirement; the individual may decide he can "stick it out." Several studies have found that successful middle-aged men think of early retirement, viewing it as a welcome release from the pressures we have discussed above. However, as the actual time approaches, many are reluctant to give up the status and authority and decide to remain until regular retirement age.

There is little research evidence that retirement is a crisis for middle-class men. Men begin to anticipate retirement and to look forward to having more unscheduled time. Bob Atchley, for example, examined work orientation among 3,704 retired teachers and telephone employees. Contrary to expectations, a high degree of work orientation was not carried into retirement by most of the people in his sample; retired women teachers were the only group who defined and evaluated themselves primarily in terms of their past work.[3]

What About Women? Middle-class women typically have had different work histories than men, and may view retirement differently. These women tend to have at least some college education and may work briefly before child-rearing brings them back to work in the home. Women begin to emerge and re-enter the labor force or school in their thirties and forties. Over half work full time when they are middle-aged, and they do so for mixed motivations of money, associations, a sense of competence, and a preparation for the independence of widowhood or divorce. They have not traditionally built careers, for they have not been expected to take career preparation seriously and arrange a series of jobs that give increasingly more responsibility and pay.

Most married women feel they must set limits on career activity so as not to interfere with family commitments. Employers often view them as "temporary" workers, no matter how long they stay. Even those who are striving in a career may reduce their commitment when they

[3] Robert C. Atchley, "Retirement and Work Orientation," *The Gerontologist* 11 (1, part 1), 1971, 29–32.

are paid less and passed over for training and promotions in favor of men. There is currently a movement to equalize career opportunities for women, particularly married women, but there are still few women who are in high level positions and who make as much money as do men.

Women always work, although much of their work is unpaid and in the home. When women enter the labor force, they typically are adding work rather than substituting one form for another. There is little evidence that men take over much housework when their wives re-enter the labor force. Middle-class and working-class women can seldom afford to hire a replacement in the home, particularly since even full-time workers earn an average of 60 percent of average full-time salaries of men. Women are concentrated in lower-level jobs which pay less. Until recent legal changes, women were often paid less than men for doing the same work. Thus, the financial incentives to work have not been as great for women as for men.

Very little is known about retirement for professional women, perhaps because there are relatively few of them. Some earlier writers merely assumed it would be no problem because they would return to the kitchen where they belonged. However, we can look at the emerging patterns of working women and speculate about retirement in the future.

Young women are more oriented toward combining career and motherhood than were their mothers. Few want to work while they have young children, but many educated women hope to build a satisfying and rewarding career during their adult years.

As women succeed in building careers, even if they start later than men, and as social-legal pressures open up opportunities and equal pay for women, several changes in the experiences of aging can be anticipated. Middle age will no longer represent the primary "retirement" period for women, when they lose the mothering job; this should relieve the depression of the minority of women who see mothering as their only meaningful role. Nor, however, will women have greatly increased leisure time in middle age, since they will continue working. If they start full career involvement later than do men, they probably will not be as bored or frustrated with their careers by their middle years.

Independent career development will surely reduce the risks of aging for women. Two of the greatest problems for older women are financial security and a sense of self-worth. Women who earn their own pensions and save for their old age will not be one man away from welfare; and financial independence contributes greatly to good feelings about the self.

If women become highly involved in their work, to the exclusion of other activities, they may experience retirement pain. However, it seems unlikely that women are rejecting the roles of mother, wife, friend, or homemaker in favor of work roles; rather they wish to add the career role as an important one during a period of life. Thus, retirement ends a satisfying period, but opens new possibilities.

ROLE LOST OR FREEDOM GAINED?

Perhaps as you think about retirement, images of South Sea island cruises, jet trips to India, or building model trains float through your mind. You may imagine the delicious luxury of *not* arising promptly, of not having to meet the deadlines, smile at the boss's jokes, or wear the right clothes for the job. You would like to be known as a sailor, rather than a lawyer, or a hostess rather than a teacher. You would like to follow the pleasures of the day as they come. If so, you are reacting to the ways in which work structures your life. What if the structure is gone, and you are no longer the Worker?

Work provides a social role, and often an identity: you are a bricklayer, or a radiologist, or a housewife. When you retire you will lose this role; if you have derived your basic identity from work, you may feel you have lost your identity too. The role of retiree is not a very clear social role, and you will not have the same kind of structure in your life. The release from the constraints of a social role can be seen as a terrible loss, resulting in aimlessness, lack of focus in life, anxiety and depression. However, the release can also mean great increase in personal freedom,[4] retirement and later maturity releasing persons from some very demanding early adulthood roles (e.g., parent, worker).

BE PREPARED

Whether retirement is seen as a threat or an opportunity depends upon preparations made early in life. Happy retired people generally are

[4] A point emphasized by Vern Bengston in *The Social Psychology of Aging*, Bobbs-Merrill Studies in Sociology Series (New York: The Bobbs-Merrill Company, Inc., 1973).

pursuing things they have enjoyed for years; after retirement they have the leisure and energy to do more fully what they did hurriedly before.

As a society we can do many things to make the last fifteen to twenty-five years of life more satisfying. Retirement from work should not be linked to an arbitrary chronological age. There is no reason to enforce excessive amounts of "leisure time" on one or two segments of the population: the old and the young. Leisure has meaning as a contrast from work; all work or all leisure is seldom satisfying.

Why not provide for work and leisure at all ages? Older persons and new parents should be allowed to work part time, and individuals can work full time as their energy and needs allow. Health, motivation, and economic need should determine the amount worked, not chronological age. Currently, our labor force does not have the desired degree of flexibility.

8

personal space:
is your house built on sand?

Each of us shapes the space around us to reflect ourself; from it we relate to the world. This process begins early in childhood, when stuffed animals are arranged on the bed "just so," and continues to the careful placement of a photo beside the hospital bed. We usually have the most freedom for this in our home, and we select furnishings and decorations that we feel are appropriate for us. College students object to the impersonality of dorm rooms, and try to overcome uniformity of space with posters. Some people invest a great deal of time and energy in such activities, and as their interests and preferences change, they feel compelled to redecorate their personal space. Women stereotypically are more concerned with this than men, presumably directing their creative energies and needs for individual expression into their homes rather than into careers. Like the young, the old want their personal possessions around them, and they want to maintain a personal space. With a lifetime of memorabilia, they want to have photographs, furniture, and housewares they feel comfortable with, that remind them of the life they have led.

One of the issues of aging is often how to maintain a satisfactory personal space. The housing that was necessary for a growing family is seldom right for one or two aging parents. Reduced income can make housing too costly, and failing health may make it impossible to shop, cook, and care for the home of many years. Alternatives must be found. A popular stereotype of aging is that older people are stuffed away into old-age or nursing homes, there to be neglected until they mercifully die. Actually, only 4 percent of the people over sixty-five years of age live in institutions, although this proportion increases substantially by age eighty-five.

There are a variety of special housing facilities available for older adults. "Retirement hotels" may offer a single room, furnished, with possibly a kitchenette; there may be dining rooms, libraries, meeting rooms, a nurse, and a social director. Some "leisure villages" aim at older adults by restricting children and offering house maintenance and recreational facilities. Some residences are run by religious or occupational organizations and try to attract people of similar background; others offer rooms on the open market. Homes for the aged may take only healthy older people and send them out to a nursing home to die; others provide hospital facilities in the home.

One problem with most of the options is that they involve moving. Moving itself is very stressful; it takes the individual out of a familiar environment, and it may be difficult to reestablish ties in the neighborhood. This is true at any age, but it may become harder as one becomes older. Moving also means recreating one's personal space, trying to reduce one's possessions to those most valued. Institutional settings, particularly, offer very little opportunity for individualizing personal space. Furniture and drapes are standard, designed for hygiene and easy maintenance. It is difficult to retain a sense of separateness and to present one's personalized image to others; lacking these, it becomes a problem to establish a sense of intimacy and sharing with others.

If we cannot invite a neighbor in for coffee or a drink, and "show ourselves" through our dishes and the refreshments offered, we must find other ways to reveal ourselves that do not involve high degrees of risk. Few of us tell others what we are directly; we communicate in many indirect ways through our dress, our gestures, our responses, and our personal space. The limitation of personal space does not totally deprive us of our sense of self or means to share our self with others, but it makes more difficult a process that many already find threatening.

Some will remain in their home of middle age, perhaps remodeling it to meet their needs. But even though the house remains and provides continuity with the past, the street may change. This has the effect of shrinking one's personal space, as the street on which one lives becomes strange. The poet Raymond Kresensky wrote of the slow

changes in an Iowa town; the changes would be more dramatic with
urban renewal.

Along Our Street

Raymond Kresensky

The old ladies on our street
Are leaving one by one.
Grandma Peters who sat by the window and rocked,
Year in and year out—looking at the world from
Her box of red geraniums; Miss Anna rolling
Her wheel chair through our end of town;
And the old ladies going to church on Sunday,
All dressed in black, and one with a cane;
And spry Mother Brown who hoed her garden
The day before she died;
All have gone.

The old men too, who used to sit on the porches,
Or around the pool halls, or down at the garage;
Some of the young men, and the young women too;
Have gone.

And their gardens with them, and their quaint old houses,
Until our street has been changed.
Now, all shiny and new, it does not remember
Destruction; even the trees are new.
Will the world remember the slow destruction
That has been here? On our street?

Wars come, perhaps a little kindly,
In the swiftness of their thrust,
In the sudden burst of their destruction.

But God, be kind to us who remember quietly,
Along our street, Time's slow destruction.

From *Selected Poems* by Raymond Kresensky (Francestown, New Hampshire:
The Golden Quill Press, Publishers, 1956). Copyright © 1956 Mildred Kresensky
Allen. Used by permission of Mildred K. Allen.

Current movement patterns suggest that couples go through regular stages of housing: an urban apartment with young children, a move to a suburban house during the child-rearing period, a move to smaller quarters in the suburb or the city in the postparental years, and a move to a home for the aged or a nursing home in advanced old age. Some people, of course, remain in the same neighborhood for their entire life; often these are ethnic neighborhoods in large cities.

Few older people want to live with their children, even though they may wish to live nearby. Three-generation households are not common, and they exist usually when there seem to be no alternate arrangements that the family can find or afford. The problems of maintaining personal space and individual freedom can be considerable if the older parent moves into the child's household; if grown children move into the parents' household, the younger family is likely to feel that its sense of autonomy is threatened.

What kind of housing is best as we grow older? No one kind, since chronological age alone is not an adequate predictor of needs. Older people are diverse, more so then young people. The element of *choice* in housing arrangements remains important, as is the opportunity to create a satisfying personal space. Some will want a small room in a building with many services; others prefer to remain in their housing of many years. Some, like Mr. Carpenter, prefer the independence of a home for the aged even when his daughter wants to take him in. Ann Tyler tells how Mr. Carpenter goes, "With all flags flying."

With All Flags Flying

Ann Tyler

Weakness was what got him in the end. He had been expecting something more definite—chest pains, a stroke, arthritis—but it was only weakness that put a finish to his living alone. A numbness in his head, an airy feeling when he walked. A wateriness in his bones that made

"With All Flags Flying," by Ann Tyler. © 1971 by Ann Tyler. Appeared originally in *Redbook*, June 1971. Reprinted by permission of Russell & Volkening, Inc., as agents for the author.

it an effort to pick up his coffee cup in the morning. He waited some days for it to go away, but it never did. And meanwhile the dust piled up in corners; the refrigerator wheezed and creaked for want of defrosting. Weeds grew around his rose-bushes.

He was awake and dressed at six o'clock on a Saturday morning, with the patchwork quilt pulled up neatly over the mattress. From the kitchen cabinet he took a hunk of bread and two Fig Newtons, which he dropped into a paper bag. He was wearing a brown suit that he had bought on sale in 1944, a white T shirt and copper-toed work boots. These and his other set of underwear, which he put in the paper bag along with a razor, were all the clothes he took with him. Then he rolled down the top of the bag and stuck it under his arm, and stood in the middle of the kitchen staring around him for a moment.

The house had only two rooms, but he owned it—the last scrap of the farm that he had sold off years ago. It stood in a hollow of dying trees beside a superhighway in Baltimore County. All it held was a few sticks of furniture, a change of clothes, a skillet and a set of dishes. Also odds and ends, which disturbed him. If his inventory were complete, he would have to include six clothespins, a salt and a pepper shaker, a broken-tooth comb, a cheap ballpoint pen—oh, on and on, past logical numbers. Why should he be so cluttered? He was eighty-two years old. He had grown from an infant owning nothing to a family man with a wife, five children, everyday and Sunday china and a thousand appurtenances, down at last to solitary old age and the bare essentials again, but not bare enough to suit him. Only what he needed surrounded him. Was it possible he needed so much?

Now he had the brown paper bag; that was all. It was the one satisfaction in a day he had been dreading for years.

He left the house without another glance, heading up the steep bank toward the superhighway. The bank was covered with small, crawling weeds planted especially by young men with scientific training in how to prevent soil erosion. Twice his knees buckled. He had to sit and rest, bracing himself against the slope of the bank. The scientific weeds, seen from close up, looked straggly and gnarled. He sifted dry earth through his fingers without thinking, concentrating only on steadying his breath and calming the twitching muscles in his legs.

Once on the superhighway, which was fairly level, he could walk for longer stretches of time. He kept his head down and his fingers clenched tight upon the paper bag, which was growing limp and damp now. Sweat rolled down the back of his neck, fell in drops from his temples. When he had been walking maybe half an hour he had to sit down again for a rest. A black motorcycle buzzed up from behind and stopped a few feet away from him. The driver was young and shabby, with hair so long that it drizzled out beneath the back of his helmet.

"Give you a lift, if you like," he said. "You going somewhere?"

"Just into Baltimore."

"Hop on."

He shifed the paper bag to the space beneath his arm, put on the white helmet he was handed and climbed on behind the driver. For safety he took a clutch of the boy's shirt, tightly at first and then more loosely when he saw there was no danger. Except for the helmet, he was perfectly comfortable. He felt his face cooling and stiffening in the wind, his body learning to lean gracefully with the tilt of the motorcycle as it swooped from lane to lane. It was a fine way to spend his last free day.

Half an hour later they were on the outskirts of Baltimore, stopped at the first traffic light. The boy turned his head and shouted, "Whereabouts did you plan on going?"

"I'm visiting my daughter, on Belvedere near Charles Street."

"I'll drop you off, then," the boy said. "I'm passing right by there."

The light changed, the motor roared. Now that they were in traffic, he felt more conspicuous, but not in a bad way. People in their automobiles seemed sealed in, overprotected; men in large trucks must envy the way the motorcycle looped in and out, hornetlike, stripped to the bare essentials of a motor and two wheels. By tugs at the boy's shirt and singled words shouted into the wind he directed him to his daughter's house, but he was sorry to have the ride over so quickly.

His daughter had married a salesman and lived in a plain, square house that the old man approved of. There were sneakers and a football in the front yard, signs of a large, happy family. A bicycle lay in the driveway. The motorcycle stopped just inches from it. "Here we are," the boy said.

"Well, I surely do thank you."

He climbed off, fearing for one second that his legs would give way beneath him and spoil everything that had gone before. But no, they held steady. He took off the helmet and handed it to the boy, who waved and roared off. It was a really magnificent roar, ear-dazzling. He turned toward the house, beaming in spite of himself, with his head feeling cool and light now that the helmet was gone. And there was his daughter on the front porch, laughing. "Daddy, what on *earth?*" she said. "Have you turned into a teenybopper?" Whatever that was. She came rushing down the steps to hug him—a plump, happy-looking woman in an apron. She was getting on toward fifty now. Her hands were like her mother's, swollen and veined. Gray had started dusting her hair.

"You never *told* us," she said. "Did you ride all this way on a motor- cycle? Oh, why didn't you find a telephone and call? I would have come. How long can you stay for?"

"Now . . ." he said, starting toward the house. He was thinking of the best way to put it. "I came to a decision. I won't be living alone any more. I want to go to an old folks' home. That's what I *want*," he said, stopping on the grass so she would be sure to get it clear. "I don't want to live with you—I want an old folks' home." Then he was afraid he had worded it too strongly. "It's nice *visiting* you, of course," he said.

"Why, Daddy, you know we always asked you to come and live with us."

"I know that, but I decided on an old folk's home."

"We couldn't do that. We won't even talk about it."

"Clara, my mind is made up."

Then in the doorway a new thought hit her, and she suddenly turned around. "Are you sick?" she said. "You always said you would live alone as long as health allowed."

"I'm not up to that any more," he said.

"What is it? Are you having some kind of pain?"

"I just decided, that's all," he said. "What I *will* rely on you for is the arrangements with the home. I know it's a trouble."

"We'll talk about that later," Clara said. And she firmed the corners of her mouth exactly the way her mother used to do when she hadn't won an argument but wasn't planning to lose it yet either.

In the kitchen he had a glass of milk, good and cold, and the hunk of bread and the two Fig Newtons from his paper bag. Clara wanted to make him a big breakfast, but there was no sense wasting what he had brought. He munched on the dry bread and washed it down with milk, meanwhile staring at the Fig Newtons, which lay on the smoothed-out bag. They were the worse for their ride-squashed and pathetic-looking, the edges worn down and crumbling. They seemed to have come from somewhere long ago and far away. "Here, now, we've got cookies I baked only yesterday," Clara said; but he said, "No, no," and ate the Fig Newtons, whose warmth on this tongue filled him with a vague, sad feeling deeper than homesickness. "In my house," he said, "I left things a little messy. I hate to ask it of you, but I didn't manage to straighten up any."

"Don't even think about it," Clara said. "I'l take out a suitcase tomorrow and clean everything up. I'll bring it all back."

"I don't want it. Take it to the colored people."

"Don't want any of it? But, Daddy—"

He didn't try explaining it to her. He finished his lunch in silence and then let her lead him upstairs to the guest room.

Clara had five boys and a girl, the oldest twenty. During the morning as they passed one by one through the house on their way to other places, they heard of his arrival and trooped up to see him. They were fine children, all of them, but it was the girl he enjoyed the most. Francie. She was only thirteen, too young yet to know how to hide what she felt. And what she felt was always about love, it seemed: whom she just loved, who she hoped loved her back. Who was just a darling. Had thirteen-year-olds been so aware of love in the old days? He didn't know and didn't care; all he had to do with Francie was sit smiling in an armchair and listen. There was a new boy in the neighborhood who walked his English sheepdog past her yard every mornmorning, looking toward her house. Was it because of her, or did the dog just like to go that way? When he telephoned her brother Donnie, was he hoping for her to answer? And when she did answer, did he want her to talk a minute or to hand the receiver straight to Donnie? But what would she say to him, anyway? Oh, all her questions had to do with where she might find love, and everything she said made the old man wince and love her more. She left in the middle of a sentence, knocking against a doorknob as she flew from the room, an unlovable-looking tangle of blond hair and braces and scrapes and Band-Aids. After she was gone the room seemed too empty, as if she had accidentally torn part of it away in her flight.

Getting into an old folks' home was hard. Not only because of lack of good homes, high expenses, waiting lists; it was harder yet to talk his family into letting him go. His son-in-law argued with him every evening, his round, kind face anxious and questioning across the supper table. "Is it that you think you're not welcome here? You are, you know. You were one of the reasons we bought this big house." His grandchildren when they talked to him had a kind of urgency in their voices, as if they were trying to impress him with their acceptance of him. His other daughters called long distance from all across the country and begged him to come to them if he wouldn't stay with Clara. They had room, or they would make room; he had no idea what homes for the aged were like these days. To all of them he gave the same answer: "I've made my decision." He was proud of them for asking, though. All his children had turned out so well, every last one of them. They were good, strong women with happy families, and they had never given him a moment's worry. He was luckier than he had a right to be. He had felt lucky all his life, dangerously lucky, cursed by luck; it had seemed some disaster must be waiting to even things up. But the luck had held. When his wife died it was at a late age, sparing her the pain she would have had to face, and his life had continued in its steady, reasonable pattern with no more sorrow than any other man's. His final lot was to weaken, to crumble and to die—only a secret disaster, not the one he had been expecting.

He walked two blocks daily, fighting off the weakness. He shelled peas for Clara and mended little household articles, which gave him an excuse to sit. Nobody noticed how he arranged to climb the stairs only once a day, at bedtime. When he had empty time he chose a chair without rockers, one that would not be a symbol of age and weariness and lack of work. He rose every morning at six and stayed in his room a full hour, giving his legs enough warning to face the day ahead. Never once did he disgrace himself by falling down in front of people. He dropped nothing more important than a spoon or a fork.

Meanwhile the wheels were turning; his name was on a waiting list. Not that that meant anything, Clara said. "When it comes right down to driving you out there, I just won't let you go," she told him. "But I'm hoping you won't carry things that far. Daddy, won't you put a stop to this foolishness?"

He hardly listened. He had chosen long ago what kind of old age he would have; everyone does. Most, he thought, were weak, and chose to be loved at any cost. He had seen women turn soft and sad, anxious to please, and had watched with pity and impatience their losing battles. And he had once known a schoolteacher, no weakling at all, who said straight out that when she grew old she would finally eat all she wanted and grow fat without worry. He admired that—a simple plan, dependent upon no one. "I'll sit in an armchair," she had said, "with a lady's magazine in my lap and a box of homemade fudge on the lampstand. I'll get as fat as I like and nobody will give a hang." The schoolteacher was thin and pale, with a kind of stooped, sloping figure that was popular at the time. He had lost track of her long ago, but he liked to think that she had kept her word. He imagined her fifty years later, cozy and fat in a puffy chair, with one hand moving constantly between her mouth and the candy plate. If she had died young or changed her mind or put off her eating till another decade, he didn't want to hear about it.

He had chosen independence. Nothing else had even occurred to him. He had lived to himself, existed on less money than his family would ever guess, raised his own vegetables and refused all gifts but an occasional tin of coffee. And now he would sign himself into the old folks' home and enter on his own two feet, relying only on the impersonal care of nurses and cleaning women. He could have chosen to die alone of neglect, but for his daughters that would have been a burden too—a different kind of burden, much worse. He was sensible enough to see that.

Meanwhile, all he had to do was to look as busy as possible in a chair without rockers and hold fast against his family. Oh, they gave him no peace. Some of their attacks were obvious—the arguments with his son-in-law over the supper table—and some were subtle; you had to be on your guard every minute for those. Francie, for instance, asking him questions about what she called the "olden days." Inviting him to sink unnoticing into doddering reminiscence. "Did I see Granny ever? I don't remember her. Did she like me? What kind of person was she?" He stood his ground, gave monosyllabic answers. It was easier than he had expected. For him, middle age tempted up more memories. Nowadays events had telescoped. The separate agonies and worries— the long, hard births of each of his children, the youngest daughter's chronic childhood earaches, his wife's last illness—were smoothed now into a single, summing-up sentence: He was a widowed farmer with five daughters, all married, twenty grandchildren and three great-grandchildren. "Your grandmother was a fine woman," he told Francie; "just fine." Then he shut up.

Francie, not knowing that she had been spared, sulked and peeled a strip of sunburned skin from her nose.

Clara cried all the way to the home. She was the one who was driving; it made him nervous. One of her hands on the steering wheel held a balled-up tissue, which she had stopped using. She let tears run unchecked down her face and drove jerkily with a great deal of brake-slamming and gear-gnashing.

"Clara, I wish you wouldn't take on so," he told her. "There's no need to be sad over *me*."

"I'm not sad so much as mad," Clara said. "I feel like this is something you're doing *to* me, just throwing away what I give. Oh, why do you have to be so stubborn? It's still not too late to change your mind."

The old man kept silent. On his right sat Francie, chewing a thumbnail and scowling out the window, her usual self except for the unexplainable presence of her other hand in his, tight as wire. Periodically she muttered a number; she was counting red convertibles, and had been for days. When she reached a hundred, the next boy she saw would be her true love.

He figured that was probably the reason she had come on this trip —a greater exposure to red convertibles.

Whatever happened to DeSotos? Didn't there used to be a car called a roadster?

They parked in the U-shaped driveway in front of the home, under the shade of a poplar tree. If he had had his way, he would have arrived by motorcycle, but he made the best of it—picked up his underwear sack from between his feet, climbed the front steps ramrod-straight. They were met by a smiling woman in blue who had to check his name on a file and ask more questions. He made sure to give all the answers himself, overriding Clara when necessary. Meanwhile Francie spun on one squeaky sneaker heel and examined the hall, a cavernous, polished square with old-fashioned parlors on either side of it. A few old people were on the plush couches, and a nurse sat idle beside a lady in a wheel chair.

They went up a creaking elevator to the second floor and down a long, dark corridor deadened by carpeting. The lady in blue, still carrying a sheaf of files, knocked at number 213. Then she flung the door open on a narrow green room flooded with sunlight.

"Mr. Pond," she said, "this is Mr. Carpenter. I hope you'll get on well together."

Mr. Pond was one of those men who run to fat and baldness in old age. He sat in a rocking chair with a gilt-edged Bible on his knees.

"How-do," he said. "Mighty nice to meet you."

They shook hands cautiously, with the women ringing them like mothers asking their children to play nicely with each other. "Ordinarily I sleep in the bed by the window," said Mr. Pond, "but I don't hold it in much importance. You can take your pick."

"Anything will do," the old man said.

Clara was dry-eyed now. She looked frightened.

"You'd best be getting on back now," he told her. "Don't you worry about me. I'll let you know," he said, suddenly generous now that he had won, "if there is anything I need."

Clara nodded and kissed his cheek. Francie kept her face turned away, but she hugged him tightly, and then she looked up at him as she stepped back. Her eyebrows were tilted as if she were about to ask him one of her questions. Was it her the boy with the sheepdog came for? Did he care when she answered the telephone?

They left, shutting the door with a gentle click. The old man made a great business out of settling his underwear and razor in a bureau drawer, smoothing out the paper bag and folding it, placing it in the next drawer down.

"Didn't bring much," said Mr. Pond, one thumb marking his page in the Bible.

"I don't need much."

"Go on—take the bed by the window. You'll feel better after awhile."

"I *wanted* to come," the old man said.

"That there window is a front one. If you look out, you can see your folks leave."

He slid between the bed and the window and looked out. No reason not to. Clara and Francie were just climbing into the car, the sun lacquering the tops of their heads. Clara was blowing her nose with a dot of tissue.

"*Now* they cry," said Mr. Pond, although he had not risen to look out himself. "Later they'll buy themselves a milk shake to celebrate."

"I wanted to come. I made them bring me."

"And so they did. *I* didn't want to come. My son wanted to put me here—his wife was expecting. And so he did. It all works out the same in the end."

"Well, I could have stayed with one of my daughters," the old man said. "But I'm not like some I have known. Hanging around making burdens of themselves, hoping to be loved. Not me."

"If you don't care about being loved," said Mr. Pond, "how come it would bother you to be a burden?"

Then he opened the Bible again, at the place where his thumb had been all the time and went back to reading.

The old man sat on the edge of the bed, watching the tail of Clara's car flash as sharp and hard as a jewel around the bend of the road. Then, with nobody to watch that mattered, he let his shoulders slump and eased himself out of his suit coat, which he folded over the foot of the bed. He slid his suspenders down and let them dangle at his waist. He took off his copper-toed work boots and set them on the floor neatly side by side. And although it was only noon, he lay down full-length on top of the bedspread. Whiskery lines ran across the plaster of the ceiling high above him. There was a cracking sound in the mattress when he moved; it must be covered with something waterproof.

The tiredness in his head was as vague and restless as anger; the weakness in his knees made him feel as if he had just finished some ex-hausting exercise. He lay watching the plaster cracks settle themselves into pictures, listening to the silent, neuter voice in his mind form the words he had grown accustomed to hearing now: Let me not give in at the end. Let me continue gracefully till the moment of my defeat. Let Lollie Simpson be alive somewhere even as I lie on my bed; let her be eating homemade fudge in an overstuffed armchair and growing fatter and fatter and fatter.

9

personality and self-concept: is this still me?

Our self-concept, how we see ourselves and feel about ourselves in relation to the world, is the key to how we will grow older—whether we will simply age or will truly grow. If we feel good about ourselves and see ourselves as a growing, learning person, then we will *grow* older. If, on the other hand, we have very negative feelings, or if our self-concept is based on superficial characteristics (e.g., physical appearance, sexual attractiveness, or even the kind of job), then as the years pass, we are likely to feel less good about ourselves. For a growing person, time-passing is parallel with growth of the self—you become ever more who you really are; you continue to be more self-actualizing. For the person who is not really in touch or at peace with his real, inner self, however, time-passing can be seen as loss—of who he thought he was, or what was superficially valued by himself and others. Knowledge and acceptance of self is central to growing older successfully.

As we all sense, many "selves" are experienced by each individual. What are these selves, how do they develop, and how do they change?

Public and Private. Everyone has a self that he is willing to share with others. This includes his public behavior and those characteristics and abilities that he is willing to admit to public view; often this "shared" self includes aspects which other people most like. It is like "putting your best foot forward." There is also an "inner self," made up partly of feelings and beliefs about oneself that one may not share with others. This "inner self" also includes deeper feelings and attitudes that one may hide even from oneself. Some feel that the "inner me" or the "real me" is too unacceptable to share. Others, perhaps wisely, hesitate to trust most others with too much knowledge of their innermost feelings.

Real–Ideal. Our sense of self includes both the self we wish we were—the **ideal self**—and the self as we feel we really are—the **real self.** If the real self is quite similar to the ideal self, we will probably feel good about ourselves and will have a "positive self-concept." Unfortunately, many people feel that the "real me" does not much resemble the "ideal me," and this awareness is usually painful. Even individuals who are successful in careers and are envied by others may still suffer from private feelings that they are not *really* good enough, according to their own ideal self-image. When there is a big gap between the real and ideal selves, it is necessary to revise one or both of them in order to feel better and become more self-actualizing.

Identity. The sense of identity refers to an almost subconscious core sense of being, and contains those qualities which are most central to our unique sense of ourselves. Our identity is the answer to the question "Who am I?"

The sense of identity includes an inner assurance of continuity with the past, the knowledge that we are not a totally different person today than we were last year, even though we have changed.

It also includes a continuity or sameness between the ways we experience ourselves and the ways others experience us. A person's sense of sureness about himself will be much stronger if both he and his employer see him as a dependable, creative, cooperative person.

The alternative extreme to a strong, unifying sense of identity is what Erik Erikson has termed "role confusion." This is the experience of not knowing "who I am," and is manifested by the acting out of different poses which seem called for by the occasion. This behavior is usually experienced by the individual as uncomfortable, and the person may actively try to develop a unified sense of self. A typical example is the housewife with school-age children who comes to experience herself as only playing many roles—Homer's wife, Bobby and Susan's mother, car-pool organizer, ticket seller, grocery shopper. "Where am *I?*" is the persistent question, and many search for innermost needs and abilities as a separate person.

Identity also includes a sense of gender—that core sense of being masculine or feminine in a particular culture. Gender identity affects nearly all our interactions, and influences our self-concept. Because sex provides an ascribed social role, our self-concept includes the experience of oneself as a *female* self or a *male* self.

WHAT MAKES THE WHOLE YOU?

The sense of self and identity develop through social interaction. Our *past experiences,* particularly in childhood, influence our basic views of ourselves as competent, capable of taking responsibility for our own lives, worthy of respect, acceptably masculine or feminine. Or, a person may come to view himself as basically incompetent, as one who must depend on others to tell him what to do and think and feel, as one not worthy of others' respect, or as somehow not a "real man" or a "real woman."

Some psychologists think almost all people emerge from childhood with deep-seated feelings that they are "not OK." [1] The "not OK" feelings must be recognized and dealt with before full adult functioning is possible.

Our *present experiences* also affect our self-concept. However, our present experiences are colored by the expectations we have developed from past experience. For example, people who expect people to like them usually relate in ways so that their expectations are confirmed. Or, certain individuals are "accident prone"—they just know they will fall, or fail, or be rejected, and their expectations are often met.

Present experiences are also colored by our ascribed (given) roles. For example, a mechanic will react differently to a woman who brings in a car to be fixed than to a man; he will treat her as if she didn't know anything about the car, even though she might know more than her husband. A wrinkled old man at a bar may be listened to with condescending attention, as though he couldn't possibly really understand current complexities of the stock market. Having people respond to one in a certain way all the time can affect how one sees oneself.

Our "achieved" roles will also affect our experiences. If a person becomes a noted author or entertainer, people may listen to his opinions respectfully—even if he knows nothing special about the subject under discussion. The woman who "marries well" will be

1 Thomas A. Harris, *I'm OK—You're OK* (New York: Harper & Row, 1969).

treated with more deference, respect, and admiration than if she had married a shoe clerk. A "green card" (signifying eligibility for welfare funds) may change the dentist's reception from cordial to cool.

Perhaps one of the most crucial elements in creating one's self is one's feeling of *control over one's own life chances*. Individuals who are realizing their potential and who have a positive self-concept usually feel that they have some control over the basic decisions affecting life. All people make decisions, but some people *feel* they have few alternatives available to them; they feel ruled by the circumstances of their lives.

Sometimes the limitations on choice are real, and reflect basic problems in our society. If you have had a stroke, cannot live alone, and have no spouse or children who will care for you, a nursing home may be the only "choice" currently available. A woman whose husband leaves and is unwilling or unable to provide continuing support usually has few good alternatives; if she stays home with the small children and receives welfare, she will have a marginal existence and considerable degradation; if she can find a job, she may have no way to provide adequate substitute care.

In both these instances, a wider range of social services would make a sense of individual control possible. A variety of visiting home-makers, adult "day care" centers, apartments with central dining rooms, medical care, and maid services, as well as full-service nursing homes, would mean that the stroke victim could chose which alternative is preferred. Similarly, excellent in-home, centralized, or on-the-job child care would allow the mother to retain more control over her life at a difficult time.

CHANGES OVER TIME

Because social interaction and experiences affect our sense of self, our self-concept may change as we grow older. The popular stereotypes of aging often include a shift to a more negative self-concept. Research evidence indicates that this is not necessarily so.

RESEARCH ON SELF-CONCEPT

Some studies report more negative self-concept among the middle-aged (forty to sixty) than among younger people; some report little difference. Riley[2] summarizes the research on self-concept and age with the following points:

(1) Older people in general (fifty-five and over) appear to view themselves quite positively, at least as positively as younger people do.

(2) The great majority (over 80 percent) of older people over fifty-five perceive strong points in themselves, their characters, or the ways they perform their roles, differing little from younger people in this regard.

(3) While most older people fifty-five and over also admit to various weaknesses and shortcomings in their personalities, they are less likely to do so than are younger people.

(4) Older people seem to be generally positive (or at least neutral) in their self-assessments, although individuals show considerable variation. They are no more (and possibly less) negative or ambivalent in self-conceptions than younger people are.

(5) Self-concepts seem to be favorable among those in better economic circumstances; among those living in the community rather than institutions; and among men more than women.

(6) Older people seem to feel at least as adequate as younger people in their family and other personal relationships. People fifty-five and over report fewer feelings of inadequacy in their marital relationships than do persons thirty-five to fifty-four (regardless of sex or educational level).

(7) There is little difference between old and young in mentioning lack of social skills as a shortcoming (for example, desiring to be "more tactful," "less easily hurt," "more interested in people").

RESEARCH ON "SOCIAL PERSONALITY"

The "outer," more visible aspects of personality processes seem quite stable until old age. Interests, the amount of time and energy devoted to being a worker, friend, volunteer, or spouse, and how one feels generally about life don't seem to change much from middle age to the mid-sixties or early seventies. At that time, social involvement drops off for many people as they retire and become widowed; these changes are often resisted by older people, and many healthy people

[2] Matilda White Riley and Anne Foner, *Aging and Society: Volume I: An Inventory of Research Findings* (New York: Russell Sage Foundation, 1968). Adapted with permission of the publisher.

remain involved and happy. Some adults are very involved in social activities, have lots of energy, and feel quite positive about themselves —but there are adults like this of *all* ages. There are also adults who always seem withdrawn, moody, and unhappy, or who have a few good friends and live a quiet, happy life. Thus, *age* is not a good predictor of changes in the "outer you."

INNER PERSONALITY

However, there do seem to be some normal, developmental shifts in the "inner" aspects of personality, beginning in middle age. These changes affect people in subtle ways.

Do you ever feel, with a sense of restlessness, that you are not really satisfied with your life, even though you may have all the things you *thought* you wanted? That is your inner self sending you a message that your inner needs and wishes are not being met. Have you ever agreed to meet a rich but overbearing uncle for dinner, and then "forgotten" to go? If so, your unconscious wishes were probably at work; you might consciously deny that you intended to forget, or feel very depressed after forgetting—but your behavior is influenced by those inner, covert, aspects of your personality. Often these influences may be subtle, and sometimes the inner processes are not translated directly into behavior.

These inner aspects of personality are not measurable by direct questioning of an individual, since the individual may not be consciously aware of his hidden feelings and perspectives. To assess these feelings, psychologists have rated personality functioning from long interviews with individuals, analyzing the qualitative aspects of the interview as well as the content. (They may rate the interview for such things as mood tone, level of affect or involvement in what is being said, discrepancies between the words said and the feeling of the respondent.)

Another technique for assessing this level of personality is the Thematic Apperception Test (TAT). Respondents are shown a picture with figures in an ambiguous position, and are asked to tell a story about the picture. Since the pictures have no clear "meaning," the story told reflects the person's own concerns, perceptions, fantasies, etc.

For example, one of the TAT cards used in the studies of personality changes among men forty to seventy showed a lightly clothed man climbing a vertical rope; since neither the top nor the bottom of the rope was visible, it was not clear whether the man was climbing up or down. Responses from many men, in different cultures, to this card showed some interesting age trends. In general terms men in their forties tended to tell stories about how the hero was able to carry out the project he wished. The following story is typical:[3]

> Well, I would guess that this character is an acrobat, engaged in aerial acrobatics. I'd say he is on his way up to his performance and that he is looking out over the group of spectators gathered for the performance, and it looks as though he might be happy—he doesn't look worried—he looks as though he is equipped to get the job done, mentally and physically.

Men in their fifties tended to tell stories in which they were not sure whether the rope climber would have the energy necessary to meet the challenge, although they hoped he would. The oldest men, characterized by less active and assertive ways of relating to the world, tended to give very short stories. They did not emphasize inner motivations so much as things outside themselves; for example, they might say, "He'll make it down if the rope doesn't break." These data, plus much more, are behind Neugarten's summary statement that the shift in covert, inner personality is from "active to passive modes of mastery." The following portion of an article on the developmental psychology of aging summarizes the data on changes in inner-life processes.

Inner-Life Processes

Bernice L. Neugarten

One series of investigations, reported in the book *Personality in Middle and Late Life* (Neugarten et al., 1964), focused on the individual's per-

---

[3] This story and the implications from this series of studies are from *Personality in Middle and Later Life* by Bernice Neugarten and Associates. (New York: Atherton Press, 1964).

ception of and styles of coping with the inner world of experience. Consistent age differences emerged when the investigator's attention was on such issues as the perception of the self vis-à-vis the external environment and where the respondent's statement and resolution of such issues were assessed on the basis of projective data. For example, 40-year-olds saw the environment as rewarding boldness and risk taking and saw themselves as possessing energy congruent with the opportunities presented in the outer world. Sixty-year-olds saw the environment as complex and dangerous and the self as conforming and accommodating to outer-world demands. This change was described as a movement from active to passive mastery.

Different modes of dealing with impulse life became salient with increasing age. Preoccupation with the inner life became greater; emotional cathexes toward persons and objects in the outer world seemed to decrease; the readiness to attribute activity and affect to persons in the environment was reduced; there was a movement away from outer-world to inner-world orientation. This change was described as increased *interiority*. There was also a constriction in the ability to integrate wide ranges of stimuli and in the willingness to deal with complicated and challenging situations. Differences with age appeared not only in projective test responses, but also in interview data when the investigator's attention was on latent rather than manifest content and when feeling states and modes of thought were inferred from indirect evidence. Thus, older men and women in verbalizing opinions in dogmatic terms, in failing to clarify past-present or cause-effect relationships, and in using idiosyncratic and eccentric methods of communication gave evidence of lessened sensitivity to the reactions of others and a lessened sense of relatedness to others.

Differences between the sexes appeared with age. Older men seemed more receptive than younger men of their affiliative, nurturant, and sensual promptings; older women, more receptive than younger women of aggressive and egocentric impulses. Men appeared to cope with the environment in increasingly abstract and cognitive terms; women, in increasingly affective and expressive terms. (Chiriboga and Lowenthal, 1971, reported findings that confirm these sex differences.) In both sexes, however, older people seemed to move toward more eccentric, self-preoccupied positions and to attend increasingly to the control and satisfaction of personal needs.

These findings are supported by those of other investigators who have studied samples of middle-aged and older men . . . all indicating that aging men seem to move from active involvement with the world to more introversive, passive, and self-centered positions. . . .

⤵ ⤵ ⤵

"IDENTITY CRISES"

The basic ingredients for one's identity develop gradually during childhood. During adolescence, many people focus on discovering who they really are, distinct from their parents and peers. The adolescent "task," according to Erikson, is to forge a strong sense of identity and overcome a sense of role confusion. The process of trying out possible "identities," and the agony of not knowing who one is, is often referred to as an **identity crisis**. Having developed, the core identity can guide career, mate, and life-style choices.

However, the sense of identity does not necessarily remain stable throughout adulthood. A person may have periodic "identity crises," times when the self he thinks he is is not confirmed by others. For example, the man of forty-five who is balding and grown paunchy may still retain an image of himself as a vigorous, assertive young-man-on-the-make. If he meets an attractvie young woman of twenty and converses with her, several things may happen to his sense of self. Possibly, she may respond to him *as if* he were highly attractive to her, *as if* she were not aware of any discrepancy in their ages—and she could be truthful. In any event, such an interaction would confirm his vision of himself as a dashing young man, and make him feel good about himself.

More likely, the girl would treat him with that subtle deference and unease that indicates respect rather than flirtation; if she called him "Sir," or suggested that he would find a lot in common with her father, his self-image would be jolted. Hopefully she would not be disgusted or outraged by his interest, and call him a "dirty old man."

Also, he might well discover that the girl bored him, that her lack of experience, self-preoccupation, and simplicity, which once would have charmed him, now seem hopelessly naive and unformed.

One's sense of identity may also be challenged in adulthood if the self one experiences now does not "fit" with the commitments made on the basis of a past self. It is very common for educated women in our society to experience an "identity crisis" in their thirties or forties; working-class women may be experiencing this also, reflecting their acceptance of the human liberation philosophy of indivduial needs and recognition.

The adult identity crisis of women is related to early socialization practices and the expectations held for women. Girls are encouraged to do well in school, but they also receive a very strong "message" that their primary destiny is to be a wife and mother. Until very recently, girls began to realize in high school that social achievement was more rewarded than academic achievement and career planning—and that they should not expect to do both.

Typically, a young woman married and had children and derived a sense of identity, not from her own independent achievements and interests, but from her status as wife and mother. But as she emerges from the honeymoon and the totally demanding early-childhood periods, the woman often asks, "Who Am *I*?" A life defined by service for others may not provide an adequate sense of individual identity.

Women now are going to therapists, workshops, classes, and rap groups to discover their inner sense of self. Problems arise when they find that their inner needs and preferences do not coincide with the commitments they have already made. Women often need help in creating a life-style that honors responsibilities to others, especially children, and yet also allows ample opportunity to develop and nurture a strong, positive sense of self.

The identity problems of women could be partially resolved by encouraging girls to think seriously about forging an identity during adolescence. They should avoid the dangers of "foreclosure," a premature, inadequate identity based on "taking over" someone else's identity, whether parent's or husband's. By establishing an independent sense of identity first, they could then make more realistic career, mate, and life-style commitments.

Men often experience identity crises in mid-life, often in the forties. By that time, the accumulated changes may be great enough to make the man feel that his "public self" and his "private self" are so different that he no longer knows who he really is. Several studies have found evidence of intensified "life review" at this time, and an altered perspective on "time left." Many men question whether they can honor the commitments made to an occupation, a wife, or a life-style.

A life review is not necessarily a crisis, but the man may experience it as one. Most men are not as successful as they hoped to be, and they must deal with their core sense of competence and worth. If they have problems with occasional (or chronic) impotence or unemployment, they have to deal with feelings that they may no longer be a "real male."

Identity may become an issue again at retirement, particularly for individuals who have defined themselves primarily in terms of a work role. As women "retire" from mothering, some undergo an identity crisis, as Pauline Bart illustrated, just as men *may* feel the lack of a central identity when they retire from work.

In old age, it may become difficult to incorporate multiple changes into the sense of identity. Men who feel that their core masculine identity relies on their strength and independence may find serious illness devastating to their sense of self. Women who feel that their femininity depends on their inability to figure income taxes, service the car, or support the family may suffer a crisis when forced to do all those things after a husband dies or becomes an invalid.

It is possible at any age to forge a strong sense of identity, of congruence between the "inner self," the self presented to others, and the ideal self. The challenge can even be met in old age. For example, the following excerpt from Clark Moustakas' book on loneliness illustrates the reemergence of a seventy-four-year-old man from a life "lived by other peoples' expectations of him." This man had not heeded his own inner needs, until finally he was overcome by a sense of loneliness, anger, and desperation.

The Experience of Being Lonely

Clark Moustakas

He stood in the doorway of my office, a terribly stooped old man. Pain and misery, heavy wrinkles, lined his face. He stared beyond me, fiery, piercing eyes fixed to the floor, a face filled with indescribable

From Clark E. Moustakas, *Loneliness,* © 1961, pp. 20–23. Reprinted by permission of Prentice-Hall, Inc., Englewood Cliffs, N.J.

loneliness and defeat. "Won't you come in and sit down?" I asked
gently. He entered the room, but he did not sit. He began to pace,
back and forth, back and forth. Increasingly, I felt the turbulence inside him which electrified my office with a kind of frozen tension. The
tension mounted, becoming almost unbearable. Heavy beads of per-
spiration fell from his face and forehead. Tears filled his eyes. He
started to speak several times but the words would not come. He
stroked his hair roughly and pulled at his clothing. The pacing continued.

I felt his suffering keenly, deep inside me, spreading throughout
my whole body. I remarked, "So utterly painful and lonely." "Lonely,"
he cried. "Lonely!" "Lonely!" he shouted, "I've been alone all my
life." He spoke in rasping tones, his nerves drawn taut. "I've never
been an honest person. I've never done anything I really wanted to
do, nothing I truly believed in. I don't know what I believe in anymore. I don't know what I feel. I don't know what to do with myself.
I wish I could die—how I have yearned, how I have longed for death
to come, to end this misery. If I had the courage, I would kill myself.
These headaches. I don't know how much more I can stand. I haven't
slept for months. I wake up in the middle of the night. Everything is
dark, black, ugly, empty. Right now my head is throbbing. I take pills.
I try to rest. Nothing helps. My head is splitting. I don't think I can
take this pain much longer. I wake with a start. My heart fills with
terror. My wife and children are asleep, with me in the house—but I
am entirely alone. I am not a father. I am not a husband. I'm no one.
Look! See these tears. I could weep forever. Forever. I sometimes feel
I cry for the whole world—a world that's sour and lost."

All this the old man uttered—sobbing, choking, sighing, gasping
for breath. The sounds were thick. His tongue was fastened to his
gums. Only with the greatest effort did he talk. It was almost unendurable. The lancinating physical pain and mental anguish mounted
relentlessly. There was not even a moment of suspension so we could
breathe normally and recapture our resources. His distress was cumu-
lative, increasingly exhaustive.

In his completely weakened state, unknown urges, unknown capacities, a surprising strength enabled him to continue. From the beginning he had never been a real person. It was too late now, he felt.
Nothing in life was real. For seventy-four years he had lived by other
people's descriptions of him, others' perceptions of him. He had come
to believe that this was his real self. He had become timid and shy

when he might have discovered and developed social interests. He was silent when he might have something to say. He played cards every Tuesday and attended club meetings every Thursday when he might have enjoyed being alone, or conversing with his wife, or developing an avocation or hobby. He listened to the radio and watched television every evening when he might have discovered values in music and books. He did not know his real interests and talents, his real aspirations and goals. He never gave himself time to discover himself.

He asked in agony, "Do you know what it means not to feel anything, to be completely without feeling? Do you understand what it is to know only pain and loneliness? My family doesn't understand me. They think I have these headaches because my business is failing. They think I roam the house at night, moving from bed to couch to chair to floor, because I'm worrying about my business. They think I'm worrying about new possibilities and plans. So they soften me and treat me gingerly. Husband and father must have a quiet house, so the house is quiet. He must not be upset, so he is avoided. He must not be expected to be friendly and sociable because he is passive and shy. He must be indirectly talked into doing what they want, in the right way, at the right moment. It takes careful planning. He must have sympathy, even if it's false, to be able to face the tough, competitive world outside. They cannot and will not recognize that this man they handle with kid gloves, whom they fear upsetting, whom they decide has to be coddled and manipulated into buying new clothes, a new car, a new home, all the other possessions a family feels it must have, this man does not really exist and never did. But who is he? Can't you see? I do not really exist. I am nothing. Do you know what it is not to know how you feel, not to know your own thoughts, not to know what you believe, not to know what you want, not to be sure of anything but endless pain and suffering? And everyone else takes you for granted, on already formed opinions and actions, the same words, the same ways. How do I start to live again? I'm dying and I can't stop breathing. I can't stop living."

These were the themes of our talks together—self-denial, estrangement, rejection, excruciating pain, spreading loneliness. We met eight times. In each visit, his suffering and sense of isolation increased, reaching unbelievable heights. Often, I thought: "Surely this is it. He has reached the breaking point." He seemed at the very end of his power and resources. But he kept coming until I wondered whether I had not reached the breaking point. The only thing that kept me going was the certainty that without me there would be no one. I could not give up, abandon him, even when I questioned my own strength to continue to live through our conversations and the lonely terror not expressible in words. I suffered deeply in these hours with him. Each time he came I felt on the verge of sinking into total despair. Often when he wept, there were tears in my eyes too, and when his head ached painfully, I, too, felt the pain. When he paced and pulled at himself, I felt a terrible restlessness and agitation; when he was utterly alone and lonely, I was alone and lonely too. My full, complete presence was not enough to alleviate his suffering, his self-lacerating expressions. I felt an awful loneliness and desolation as I was not able to help him find a beginning, locate a direction, a new pathway of relatedness to himself and others. It hurt me deeply to see him grow increasingly, unbelievably tortured and not be able to help him find a meaning or even some beginning belief in the possibility of a good life. He was dying before me and something within me was dying too. I could not reach him. I do not know what the effort of will power, what inner strivings of the heart, what forces kept me going in the face of this unendurable, mounting desolation, despair, and loneliness. I felt defeated and weakened, yet each time he came I met him squarely, honestly, directly. Each time my capacity for bearing with him seemed to be reaching a terminal point, new threads inside revived me. Somehow fresh strength flowed into me, mysteriously, encouraging me and enabling me to continue. I listened to him and believed in him. I was convinced he had the power within himself to find a new meaning in life. I continued to live with him in the crucial hours of psychic dying. My entire office filled with his aching. I could feel it everywhere in the room, in the floor, the walls, the furniture, the papers and books on my desk. It settled irrevocably and was stationary. For some time after he left, I did not move. I remained heavy as the feeling he left when he departed.

Then on the ninth appointment he did not come. What could this defection mean? How had I failed? Had he sensed my own growing struggle, my own exhaustion, my own loneliness? I searched within myself and within our relation but I could find no satisfactory answer.

Two weeks passed before he called. He spoke in a calm voice, in a totally different way from any previous words. "It's all so fresh and raw," he said, "and so new and startling that I'm constantly uncertain, but I feel I am coming into a totally new existence. I sometimes doubt that what I am feeling will last, but the feelings have persisted now almost two weeks and I'm beginning to recognize them as my own. I do not know what is happening or how, but by some strange miracle or inner working, I am beginning to breathe again and to live again. I do not want to see you just now because I must have further confirmation, but I will call you soon."

Six weeks later the old man came for the last time. I could barely recognize him. He looked youthful. His face was alive. His smile was radiant and so thrilling I felt tingling sensations everywhere inside me. He spoke warmly, confidently, "I came only to see your face light up, to be warmed by the gleam in your eyes. I know how much you suffered. I have seen your tortured face even after leaving you. I'll just sit here with you quietly a few minutes." So we sat in silence, each revelling in the birth, each warmed by a bond that emerged from deep and spreading roots in the hours of anguish and loneliness. We were no longer alone or lonely. We had found a new strength and sustenance in each other.

The fundamental communion in which we suffered enabled him to get to the very depths of his experience. Perhaps in arriving at the foundation of his grief and loneliness, immediate death or immediate life were the only choices within reach. He chose to live. From his rock bottom loneliness emerged a new life and a real self was restored.

DEVELOPING PERSONAL POTENTIALS

How can we develop a positive sense of ourselves that will be resilient in the face of all the changes to come? One major element in doing so is to begin to recognize our own needs and meet them.

Maslow's concept of a hierarchy of needs is valuable in understanding adult behavior.[4] He saw human behavior as motivated by needs at various levels. The most basic needs are for physiological comfort (food, rest, warmth, etc.), and safety (security, freedom from fear). Belongingness and love needs emerge when, and only if, the first two are met. Esteem needs are the next level, and they include the desire for competence and prestige. Finally, if these needs have been met, a new restlessness may develop "unless the individual is

[4] Abraham H. Maslow, *Motivation and Personality* (New York: Harper Brothers, 1970), Second Edition.

doing what he, individually, is fitted for"; this Maslow called the need for self-actualization.

The higher-level needs are less related to sheer survival, are less urgent, produce more profound feelings of happiness when met, and require better outside conditions to make meeting them possible. The needs, once met, do not necessarily stay satisfied forever; divorce can make belongingness needs most important, and poverty can make it impossible to be concerned with much else beyond the next meal.

At a social level, we must strive to meet the lower-level human needs for survival and safety, by making comfortable housing, good food and medical care, and protection from physical harm basic "rights" of every citizen. Individuals would then be able to focus on meeting their higher-level needs.

These can best be met by developing a sense of identity that incorporates the full range of human qualities. Human beings have a rich variety of needs, emotions, and abilities. Self-actualizing people are able to acknowledge, appreciate, and use all their attributes. This means creating a *human* identity rather than a traditionally masculine or feminine identity.

Traditional male and female identities are confining, and make it difficult to integrate outer and inner selves. An identity based on the "masculine ideal" in our culture makes it difficult to admit and meet needs for nurturance and dependency and to use abilities of empathy, tenderness, and compassion. An identity based on our cultural expectations of femininity denies the assertive, competent, competitive aspects of human potential, and makes it very difficult to meet needs for esteem, recognition, and self-actualization.

In addition, by accepting a wider range of human qualities as "ideal," it is much more likely that your "real self" will coincide with your "ideal self." By not ruling out any qualities and needs arbitrarily, you are free to be aware of your inner needs and to meet them without guilt. You can share the real you with others and not fear that, for example, you're not a "real woman" if you admit you are angry at being assumed ignorant by the auto mechanic.

Self-actualizing people incorporate both "masculine" and "feminine" strengths. They make the best and fullest use of their abilities. For example, the most intellectually competent, creative men (and boys) tend to be those with more "feminine" qualities, and the most intellectually competent women (and girls) are those who are more "masculine." [5] They can use "feminine intuition" and "masculine analysis" to understand and solve problems. They can be assertive, nurturant, and acknowledge dependency—in response to a particular situation and not to general stereotype norms of "proper" male or female behavior. Such men and women are acknowledging and using more of their *human* attributes.

Learning to recognize and meet one's own needs is not selfish, but essential. A fully self-actualizing person can reach out to others and help meet their needs, and will be able to have a broad perspective for the welfare of the whole society. People who are able to make the choices that best meet their own needs, and not necessarily those that their parents or others imposed on them, will be happier, more fulfilled, and more capable of providing for the next generation the best possible role model for aging.

[5] Eleanor Maccoby, "Sex Differences in Intellectual Functioning," in *The Development of Sex Differences,* Edited by Eleanor Maccoby (Stanford, Cal.: Stanford University Press, 1966), pp. 25-55.

10

successful aging: adding years to our lives?

"To grow old gracefully—is not to grow old." Such is the somewhat cynical statement which summarizes one point of view; many of the young and middle-aged would agree with it. Success at any age is not easy to define. Against what standard do we measure success? Are some people more successful in coping with changes related to age than others? Several definitions are possible, depending on the emphasis.

WHAT IS SUCCESS?

Survival is one definition of successful aging. The "survival of the fittest" principle implies that those who die younger are less fit. This makes some sense; biologically, the survivors into old age are superior (omitting the effect of accidents and murders). Survivors seem to be intellectually superior to nonsurvivors. Looking at personality attributes of very old people who survived institutionalization in a home for the elderly, it appears that one does *not* grow old gracefully. The survivors tended to be suspicious, hostile, aggressive, demanding, egocentric—qualities which would be termed pathological in a middle-aged person, but which were evidently functional in institutionalized elderly.[1] This finding would fit in with the explanation of some elderly

1 Barbara F. Turner *et. al.,* "Personality Traits as Predictors of Institutional Adaption Among the Aged," *Journal of Gerontology,* 27 (1), January, 1972, pp. 61–68.

behavior. The complaining, the trouble-recounting behavior of many elderly persons may be perpetuated because they are rewarded with social interaction when they complain. The more unpleasant the dependent aged person is, the more he is rewarded by the very people who are annoyed by his complaining. Persons in institutional settings, such as homes for the elderly, may feel they must resort to extreme behavior—often negative—to gain attention.

A more social definition of success is *maintenance of middle-aged patterns* of social activity. Given this definition, seventy-year-olds who look like fifty-year-olds in terms of activity and involvement can be termed more "successful" at resisting or ignoring age. This perspective has been termed the "activity theory" of successful aging, and is the underlying assumption behind most Golden Age clubs, social programs for senior citizens, and the behavior of highly active individuals.

A personalized definition of success in aging is *how the person feels.* Is the person happy? Is his morale good? If the individual thinks he is happy, is he not "successful"? We can also use a more psychiatric definition of successful aging, namely, *ability to deal with change in nondestructive ways.*

Adjustment as a standard of mental health is ambiguous, for who is to judge whether the individual should adjust to the change, or whether it is healther to resist and change a destructive situation?

The measurements used to assess successful aging reflect the theory and assumptions behind them. It is always important to discover what meaning and what measure of "success" was used when evaluating any prescription for a ripe old age.

RESEARCH ON ADJUSTMENT

Research on life satisfaction as related to age has been summarized by Matilda White Riley.[2] As the stereotype indicates, satisfaction *generally* diminishes with advancing age. However, if we look at specific reactions,

> older people appear to differ from younger people not so much in levels of satisfaction as in the kinds of gratifications and anxieties experienced

2 From "Life Satisfaction" in *Aging and Society, Vol. I: An Inventory of Research Findings,* by Matilda White Riley and Anne Foner (New York: Russell Sage Foundation, 1968).

and regarded as important. The typical older person is not only as likely as a younger person to have a sense of adequacy and worth, but also as likely to seem content with his occupational and familial roles and to encounter no greater problems in them. And despite the objective difficulties confronting the older person, he appears even less likely to worry. Thus, the older a person is, the more nearly he seems to have come to terms with the specific conditions of his life.

Aging, then, brings greater acceptance of reality.

Satisfaction among the elderly has been correlated with a variety of factors over the past years. Findings are both consistent and inconsistent, as David Adams has pointed out.[3] Health, socioeconomic status, and social relations are consistently related to satisfaction. Findings regarding retirement and satisfaction are ambiguous, with some more satisfied after retirement and some less satisfied.

Personality factors associated with successful aging have been investigated in some 2,000 "normal" (noninstitutionalized) adults over a period of ten years at the University of Chicago. Bernice Neugarten summarizes these studies. She also discusses, briefly, the *disengagement theory* of successful aging, which was developed, tested, and modified on the basis of the systematic research.

Successful Aging

Bernice L. Neugarten

One of our lines of research has been focused on the question of *successful* aging. Without going into a long recounting of a story that is familiar to many students of gerontology, the disengagement theory, and then a major modification of the theory, emerged from our Chicago group. When first stated in the early 1960s, it set off a controversy in the field that lasted 10 years; a controversy that has now

[3] David Adams, "Correlates of Satisfaction Among the Elderly," *The Gerontologist*, 11 (4, part 2), Winter, 1971, 64–68.

Edited from "Personality and the Aging Process" by Bernice L. Neugarten, the 1971 Robert W. Kleemeier Award Lecture delivered at the 24th Annual Meeting of the Gerontological Society, and printed in *The Gerontologist*, Spring, 1972. Used by permission of the author and The Gerontological Society.

abated, largely, as I like to think, because of some of our own work regarding personality.

The first statement of the theory was based on a recognition of the significance of our findings regarding intrapsychic psychological changes, especially the fact that these changes seemed to precede changes in social behavior. It was observed that as people grow old, their social interaction decreases; but looking at the psychological changes, it was postulated that the decrease in social interaction is characterized by mutuality between society and the aging person—the person has decreasing emotional involvement in the activities that characterized him earlier and thus withdraws from those activities. As a second part of the theory, it was proposed that in old age the individual who has disengaged is the person who has a sense of psychological well-being and will be high in life satisfaction.

Some of us were uncomfortable with this second part of the theory. As we gathered more data and as we studied the lives of the people in our sample, we did not find the consistent patterns that were predicted from the disengagement theory. Something seemed wrong. Therefore, once all the Kansas City data were in, we devised new and better measures of social interaction and of psychological well-being than the ones originally formulated. Now we found that high life satisfaction was more often present in persons who were socially active and involved than in persons who were inactive and uninvolved. This finding has since been confirmed in our pilot study of men aged 70-75 in six industrialized countries.

More important, we found diversity. Some people were high-high on the two sets of variables; some, high-low; some, low-low; and some, low-high. Noting that the disengagement theory could not account for this diversity, we asked, how could it be accounted for?

By that time we had worked out, with the aid of sophisticated statistical techniques, a set of empirically derived personality types. Now, in assessing all three kinds of data on each person—extent of his social interaction, degree of life satisfaction, and personality type—we found a high degree of order in the data. Certain personality types, as they age, slough off various role responsibilities with relative comfort and remain highly content with life. Other personalities show a drop in role and in social interaction and show a drop in life satisfaction. Still others have long shown low levels of activity accompanied by high satisfaction and show relatively little change as they age. For instance, in one group of 70- to 79-year-olds, persons who were living in the community and carrying out their usual daily rounds of activities, we empirically derived eight different patterns of aging. We attached the names, Reorganizers, Focused, Disengaged, Holding-on, Constricted, Succorance-seeking, Apathetic, and Disorganized, each name conveying something of the style of aging common to each of the subgroups.

We have concluded from this line of studies that personality organization or personality type is the pivotal factor in predicting which individuals will age successfully and that adaptation is the key concept.

Furthermore, although we lack systematic longitudinal data to confirm this view, it has appeared from the life-history information available on the people we studied that the patterns reflect long-standing life styles and that consistencies rather than inconsistencies in coping styles predominate as an individual moves from middle age through old age. Within broad limits—given no major biological accidents or major social upheavals—patterns of aging are predictable from knowing the individuals in middle age. (This conviction has led us at Chicago, naturally enough, to expand our perspective on the field of aging to include middle age and then young adulthood: in short, to conceive of a broader time-span, adulthood, as the relevant one for studying aging.)

In demonstrating that there is no single pattern by which people grow old, and in suggesting that persons age in ways that are consistent with their earlier life-histories, it is our view that given a relatively supportive social environment, older persons like younger ones will choose the combinations of activities that offer them the most ego-involvement and that are most consonant with their long-established value patterns and self-concepts. Aging is not a leveler of individual differences except, perhaps, at the very end of life. In adapting to both biological and social changes, the aging person continues to draw upon that which he has been, as well as that which he is.

In giving central importance to personality factors and to the continuities in personality, and in seeing people as active rather than passive, this is not to underestimate the importance of various social, economic, and biological conditions. We know, of course, that if minimum levels of life satisfaction are to be achieved, people need enough money to live on, and decent housing, and health services, and an environment that provides opportunities for social interaction. From this perspective, a major research problem for social scientists interested in successful aging will continue to be that of elucidating the economic, political, and social conditions that are associated with psychological well-being for older people.

At the same time, variations in socio-cultural contexts will not solve the problem of individual variation—that is, why some individuals are more content than others who live in the same social setting. Despite the likelihood that some settings will be found to provide greater freedom and permissiveness for a broad range of life styles, that some will be found to provide greater pressures for social participation, some, greater economic benefits, and so on, we shall still need to look at the ways individual older people adapt to the settings in which they find themselves.

It is the manner in which the individual deals with a variety of contingencies in his life—some of them social, some of them biological —which will continue to be the second important research issue. What does an old person make of his world, and how is the adaptational process influenced by his past life-history and his expectations? In attempting to understand why one individual copes successfully with retirement while another does not, or with illness, we shall have to pursue in much greater depth the ways in which aging individuals relate their pasts with their presents, how they reconcile expectations with reality, and how they interpret and integrate their lives into meaningful wholes.

Humans have, as Neugarten points out, great capacity to integrate their past and present. People reinterpret their lives into meaningful wholes.

This means that we must conceptualize adjustment as a balance of positives and negatives. Life will always be full of strife, anxiety, and challenge. These can be experienced as paralyzing or as creating opportunities for growth. It is easy to overemphasize in stereotype either the presumed positive attributes or the negative characteristics of any particular group—whether they be carefree youth or lonely old people. Individuals experience things both positively and negatively. Overall adjustment may depend on the relative strength of positive, negative, and neutral feelings. For example, Helen Lawrence Brown, poetess (and mother of musician Oscar Brown, Jr.), writes of "The very special joys of elderly ladies."

The Very Special Joys of Elderly Ladies

Helen Lawrence Brown

Elderly ladies all are agreed that
Old age has many lamentations.
It also has some compensations—
For example:
You no longer have to mind your image
Or be a model, for
No one is depending on you for direction.
You don't have to prove anything about
Your character
Your attitudes or
Your morals.
You can even see an X-rated movie, if you like,
And no one will think you're going astray.
Or read "The Sensuous Woman"
Without covering the book jacket,
Altho you'd probably be bored to tears
with both of them.
Nobody cares if you, sometimes, go to market
With a run in your stocking
or wearing last year's hat.

Little is required of you, socially,
Except that you be neat and pleasant and don't whine.
Someone always helps you up the stairs
And even down if the steps are steep.
If you should stumble
or bump into anyone.
They even pretend it was really not your fault,
Altho you know they're wondering

Why that poor soul doesn't look where she's going.
Nice young girls will read price tags for you,
If you should go shopping without your glasses.
No more do you have to fill out
complicated application forms
Or struggle to select the right answer
for multiple choice examinations.
You're out of the running,
and accept the fact with grace.
Often a young granddaughter tells you
"You look pretty today"
And you know she means
That very special kind of pretty
Reserved for grandmothers
In little girls' hearts—
And you feel rewarded.
The most comfortable chairs are saved for you.
And if on rare occasions someone is unkind,
You no longer feel the need to voice resentment.
For with the years comes compassion
And you find yourself truly sorry for
The person who felt the *need* to be unkind.
Now I ask you, who else could ever
Know such riches; such joy?
Except, of course, all of the other
Elderly ladies you know!

Mrs. Brown obviously enjoys many of the "compensations" of old age. Probably you will find different gratifications in old age. Each of us is the most important determinant of our own happiness and adjustment. What would make one person depressed may be quite satisfying to another.

For example, popular stereotypes associated social isolation with unhappiness and both with old age. However, a study of community residents and hospitalized older people showed that lifelong isolation was not necessarily associated with maladaption in later life. The findings suggested that "the former self rather than reference groups or individuals, may increasingly become the salient yardstick for the sense of relative deprivation in old age." [4]

4 Marjorie Fisk Lowenthal and David Chiriboga, "Social Stress and Adaptation: Toward a Life-Course Perspective," In *The Psychology of Adult Development*

Individuals who have never been intimately involved with others or socially active do not seem to experience deprivation in old age. But people who have had many friends and activities in middle age and lose them in old age will experience deprivation. They may still objectively be more active in the community, have more friends, and receive more attention from their families than most of their neighbors, but if these activities represent a substantial decrease from their own middle-aged patterns, they may subjectively feel deprived and unsatisfied.

Some people experience losses of close relationships as relief. Morton Hunt, for example, tells of some divorced men and women who realized that they were never really comfortable with the demands of intimacy. They find the "loss" comforting, sometimes to their own surprise.[5] Changes in amount or quality of social interaction are not, then, always experienced as painful.

These findings imply the importance of variety in understanding successful aging. The notion of "different strokes for different folks" applies for older as well as younger people.

Continuity and Change. It appears that continuity with the past is important to good adjustment for most people. For example, a two-year longitudinal study of older people involuntarily relocated into a noninstitutional residential public housing facility indicated that high adjustment at the end of the study period was associated with maintained continuity in patterns of activity. Adjustment was also aided by substituting activities for those lost. Low levels of adjustment were associated with discontinuity in activity patterns and no substitution for the lost activities.[6]

Toffler, in considering ways of handling "future shock," indicates that successful adaptation can occur only when the level of stimulation, or amount of change and novelty in the environment, is neither too low nor too high.[7] However, the determination of the optimum amount of change is, understandably, difficult. Undoubtedly individuals differ greatly in their adaptive range; probably the desired ratio between change and stability is a personality characteristic.

and Aging, edited by Carl Eisdorfer and M. P. Lawton (Washington, D.C.: American Psychological Association, 1973), p. 287.

[5] Morton Hunt, *The World of the Formerly Married* (New York: McGraw-Hill, Inc., 1966).

[6] Betty Havens, "An Investigation of Activity Patterns and Adjustment in An Aging Population," *The Gerontologist,* 8(1), 1968, 201–6.

[7] Alvin Toffler, *Future Shock* (New York: Bantam Books, 1971).

Human adaptation is affected by both the social situation and individual personality attributes. Lawton and Nahemow[8] have proposed a model for understanding adaptation and stress. Stress is subjectively experienced and adaptive behavior becomes inadequate when the environmental press (demands) are either much less than or much more than the individual's abilities to cope with the demands. Thus, stress can be alleviated either by lowering levels of environmental demands or by increasing individual competence to deal with the demands; an ideal social intervention program would use both strategies where possible.

The important point is that individuals need both continuity and change, and that each individual must determine what balance is comfortable for him. Social policies should be directed at making it possible for individuals to maintain their desired ratio of change and stability.

Insofar as Toffler is correct about the continued rapid pace of social, cultural, and technological change, one important preparation is to remain able to adapt to these changes. Toffler recommends anticipation of the direction and rate of change. It is also important to use this ability to anticipate results to resist those changes which will have consequences more negative than positive. Toffler suggests that "if we opt for rapid change in certain sectors of life, we can consciously attempt to build stability zones elsewhere." [9]

IMPLICATIONS

The implications of this information are several. First, much more research is needed on the ways individuals develop the coping styles they use throughout life. From a humanistic perspective, mere survival is not a sufficient criterion of successful aging. While it has been a major accomplishment in the past to survive a century, this will be more common in the future. As the novelty diminishes, so does the social status which accompanies any rare occurrence. The quality of the years lived becomes increasingly important, as control over our destinies becomes technologically possible. The emphasis needs to be on maximizing the human potential, not on mere absence of pathology.

8 M. P. Lawton and L. Nahemow, "Ecology and the Aging Process," in C. Eisdorfer and M. P. Lawton, eds., *The Psychology of Adult Development and Aging* (Washington, D.C.: The American Psychological Association, 1973), esp. pp. 657–66.
9 *Op. cit.*, p. 379.

You may wish to resist changes in personal relationships and work for stability and continuity there. Human potential seems best served not by many superficial, role-specific relationships, but by lasting intimate relationships. An old person is happier (and in better mental health) with one good long-time friend who will share confidences than with a dozen acquaintances at the Senior Citizens center.

Of course, intimate, close relationships hold more potential for pain as well as satisfaction; they require more nurturance than short-term, limited friendships. The disposable friendship has an appeal similar to disposable cans and tablecloths. The effects of this impermanence in people as well as things leads to a kind of superficiality and lack of commitment that is undesirable. Commitment is necessary to accomplish anything of lasting value.

Successful aging means accepting the consequences of choices made; Erikson speaks of the sense that "it was the best life it could have been." Choices always leave a residue of doubt—was the choice made the best one? What would have happened if you had traveled the other road? As we look back upon our lives, we too may ponder "The road not taken."

The Road Not Taken

Robert Frost

Two roads diverged in a yellow wood,
And sorry I could not travel both
And be one traveler, long I stood
And looked down one as far as I could
To where it bent in the undergrowth;

Then took the other, as just as fair,
And having perhaps the better claim,
Because it was grassy and wanted wear;
Though as for that, the passing there
Had worn them really about the same,

And both that morning equally lay
In leaves no step had trodden black.

Oh, I kept the first for another day!
Yet knowing how way leads on to way,
I doubted if I should ever come back.

I shall be telling this with a sigh
Somewhere ages and ages hence:
Two roads diverged in a wood, and I—
I took the one less traveled by,
And that has made all the difference.

In his poem, Frost showed an acceptance of his life as it had been. Most psychologists would see this as a successful way to approach life's end.

OLDEST AGE: WHEN THE END IS NEAR

If we are to look for secrets of successful aging, we must consider advanced old age. There is much evidence that we can arrange our lives to manage well after middle age. But the period termed *old* is often accompanied by serious illnesses, disorientation, and accumulated losses that overwhelm the ability to remain independent. Most of us do not anticipate this with pleasure. We may wonder what can possibly constitute "success" under such conditions.

It is possible to delay very old age, but not to deny it completely. Successful old age may mean dying in dignity. Elisabeth Kübler-Ross[10] has shared the thoughts of the dying. From her work, and from that of others, several issues in very old age have become clear. The process of dying is more fearful than death itself. As we approach death, we may wonder whether we will be in pain, whether we will be alone or with a friend. We wonder how we will bear up to this last challenge: will we be whiny and cantankerous and irritate those with us? Can we look back on our lives and feel that we did the best we could? Will we still be angry with ourselves or with others? More threatening yet, will

[10] Elisabeth Kübler-Ross, *On Death and Dying* (New York: The Macmillan Company, 1969).

we die as vegetables, shells of our former selves, unseeing and unknowing? The prospect of losing control over mind, bowels, and feelings is a dreadful one.

To die in dignity, most of us want to control our passage. We may wish to resist the "conspiracy of silence" and seek out those who are comfortable talking with us about our feelings and last wishes; most in our culture are yet as poorly prepared to do this. We may wish to die before we become inhuman, a resented burden on our families; if so, it will be necessary to make clear while we are still healthy that we do not want medical intervention simply to preserve technical life. When the time comes to die, we might prefer to be in our own personal, familiar space, surrounded by things which will help orient us to our life. At the very end, there is little the sterile hospital can do to ease one's passing. Most persons would probably appreciate companionship, and relief from pain; hypnosis, drugs, wine and music—all may help. There is a time to live, and a time to die.

11

new perspectives: adding life to our years

Biological advances are adding years to our lives. The challenge now is to add *life* to our years. How can we do this?

There are some things that each of us can do that will prepare us for aging. For instance, we can examine our own feelings about aging and the elderly. We can read more about aging, and challenge the assumptions we may have held. We can learn to approach people openly, without preconceptions of age, and then be enabled to discover their wisdom, skills, and vulnerabilities. You can learn much more about growing older than this book can tell you by really *listening* to older people, visiting them where they live, work, and play, and empathizing with their experiences.

On the basis of the materials presented in this book, we can delineate some of the personal qualities that seem to be associated with "successful" aging—that is, with becoming more self-actualizing as one grows older.

It is important to *recognize and accept inner needs,* and to learn how best to meet those needs. Only when these inner needs are met can the "inner self" and the "outer self" be brought into a harmonious, integrated whole. Individuals who can meet their own "lower-level needs" can then work on meeting "higher-level needs" of esteem, recognition, and self-actualization. Individuals who can accept their own inner needs should also be able to accept the inner needs of *others* as legitimate and important.

Enthusiasm and zest for living are qualities much admired in adults of all ages. The person who can keep alive a sense of discovery and a desire for life-long learning will rarely suffer from boredom. The sense of joy is often aided by a sense of humor, an ability to enjoy incongruity and surprise, and to keep a sense of perspective.

Mental flexibility rather than mental rigidity is related to continuous learning and the ability to adapt to inevitable social changes. Mental acuity is lost if not used, and there are many opportunities to develop and pursue interests throughout life, in lectures, workshops, classes, discussion groups, reading, etc. Many of these are offered through local colleges and high schools; often individuals get together and find an instructor. Individuals who age well are willing to make the effort necessary to be open to new learning, and to revise prior beliefs and skills to be more suited to current realities.

Related to this is the ability to be flexible in targets of emotional investment—some called it *cathectic flexibility*. Since friends, relations, and causes may pass away as time goes on, well-adapting individuals are able to invest their attention, love, and enthusiasm in new interests.

Successful agers have a sense of *generativity*—an investment in the future, and a sense of continuity with the past. Their lives gain meaning from a sense of being a link in a continuing chain of past, present, and future. They may focus the sense of continuity within the family; they may acknowledge the importance of preserving a life worth living for generations to come. This provides a sense of purpose for leaving the world a better place then when they entered.

By providing a vision of continuing life, a sense of generational continuity enables one to *appreciate the experiences available at every stage in life.* Well-aging individuals do not try to cram all of life into the first three decades and then despair at the "nothingness" to come. They are not interested in perpetual youth or arrested development, but in developing and enjoying the full experiences of each period in life.

Self-actualizing people are *able to make commitments,* and accept the responsibilities of the choices they have made. The commitment may be to friends; a confidante relationship is important in old age. The commitment may also be to values and ethical standards.

Commitment involves taking positive action to preserve values and rights when they are threatened, rather than showing passive resistance to change. Commitment may mean joining with others and working for social changes that will help older adults. Some changes will come only through legislative or legal action. The treatment of older Americans is a political issue, at every level of government; you can become aware of the position taken by various elected officials, and campaign for those who will work for changes you want.

There are many issues in aging with which you may want to become personally involved. The following seem to be critical areas for improvement.

(1) **Support gerontology.** Gerontology, the study of adult development and aging, is a comparatively new field, and will become increasingly important. One aspect of this field is *basic research,* focused on formulating and testing hypotheses about age-related changes in human behavior. Much of the research cited in this book is of this kind, and it is necessary to advance our understanding of aging processes so as to learn how best to help people as they age. The research needs to focus on positive adaptive capacities as well as problems of development. Biological research is crucial to combat many of the negative aspects of aging.

We also need to train professionals to work with older adults. A life-cycle perspective, emphasizing changes over time throughout adulthood, should be encouraged in all "helping professionals" (such as social workers, health-care workers, recreation workers, educators, personnel managers, psychotherapists, etc.). We need more people trained in direct services to the elderly, since they can provide alternatives to isolation or institutionalization, or can make nursing-home care more humane. The status and pay of such workers should reflect the important services they offer—services which will, hopefully, be available to *us* as we need them.

You may want to consider gerontology as a career field. If you are a scientist and "discoverer," you might want to do research in this area; it is an exciting, fast-developing discipline. You may want to provide services, or work at a political level for desirable changes. Most good universities now offer courses in gerontology.

(2) **Financial security** is the most crucial issue for aging Americans, and it is likely to be an issue for all of us, to, as we grow older. Many of the poor are elderly. Some of them worry about meeting basic survival needs. The majority of the elderly are not poor, but they experience a decreased standard of living.

There is a minimum income necessary to participate in the social system in later years, as in the earlier ones. If you cannot afford a telephone, you lose a valuable link with the outside world. If you cannot

buy a dress, invite a friend over who has had you to dinner, or contribute to your favorite charity, it is hard to retain your social roles. It
requires money to enjoy increased leisure, whether through world
travel or a bus ride to visit your granddaughter. Healthy foods are
expensive; the alternative may be depression, disorientation, and dizzi-
ness caused not by old age but by malnutrition.

Social Security benefits are not yet adequate to live on; some can
survive on them. (Find out what the benefits would be for you now,
and try to live on that amount.) The Social Security system is good
because benefits are given to all who are covered, as a matter of right.
The recipients feel that they have earned them by prior years of productivity; they are receiving deferred payment, not charity. Unfortunately, wives tend to be penalized under the Social Security system.
Benefits are based on years in the paid labor force and amount of
money earned (with only part of the income "counted"). Women who
work sporadically, and in low-paying jobs, receive little or no Social
Security benefits of their own. Women who work in the home are not
covered at all, and they may be left with no independent source of income in old age; this is particularly a problem for women who are
divorced in the later years and whose husbands remarry. Thus, while
the system is an excellent start, and while many inequities have been
corrected thus far, Social Security coverage should be expanded if it is
to indeed provide a "floor" basic guaranteed income for all older persons.

Private pensions are currently very unreliable sources of income
for most elderly. Such benefits cover relatively few workers, are often
lost if jobs are changed, typically provide minimal or no benefits to
surviving spouses, and are generally inadequate even when received.
You may wish to inquire about pension benefits on your job, and work
within the company, union, or professional association to improve
them.

One of the basic issues of financial security is whether we, as a
society, believe that adequate incomes, health care, and decent housing
are the right of every member of society—or only of those who are currently productive in ways the society values at the time. Our actions
tend to reflect the latter viewpoint, and they contribute to the uncomfortable position of the elderly.

To more equitably distribute the wealth of our society we can
provide direct services—such as subsidized housing, free medical care,
food stamps, reduced carfare for the elderly—or we can provide addi-

tional money with which to purchase these services. One well-run program combines both—the Green Thumb program uses federal (tax) money to hire older rural workers to do community-service jobs; they also receive some direct benefits, such as hot meals and medical care.

Perhaps you can investigate opportunities like this in your community. Try to anticipate how you will feel when you are older—would you prefer higher Social Security payments, or special "senior citizen" rates on medical care, food, housing, movies, etc.? They might have similar effects on maintaining your standard of living, but they may have very different psychological consequences.

(3) **Reduce agism.** Agism is a fairly powerful force in our society, operating to the detriment of all. Agism restricts our freedom to manage our own destiny, since some social roles may be denied or rigidly enforced because of age.

You can begin with some consciousness-raising—examining your own behavior and that of those around you for unconscious, perhaps subtle, bias in the way you treat people of different ages. What *assumptions* do you and others make about older people, without testing them for reality?

You can encourage the examination not only of unconscious bias and personal behavior, but of institutional practices which have the *effect* (even if not the stated intent) of discriminating against certain age groups. For example, flexibility in employment practices is very desirable. Parents of young children and older people, especially, should be able to work on a part-time basis—without taking substantial cuts in job level, pay, and fringe benefits. Retirement should not be mandatory by age, but work involvement at *all* ages should be related to energy, abilities, productivity, job requirements, and desires. (Some people are ready to "retire" at thirty, and others are productive workers at eighty.)

Workers should be able to change jobs to meet changing abilities —the aging factory worker might be able to continue working, but on a slower production line. We can assume that many workers would like to shift careers, and a person should not be automatically rejected as "too old" at forty or fifty to start in a new field. Personnel practices, including recruitment, hiring, promotion, and retirement, should not deny opportunity on the basis of age.

Higher educational institutions have traditionally been guilty of agism. With the assumption that you *can't* teach an old dog new tricks, many universities have, for example, denied admission to anyone over

30 (for Ph.D. or medical school programs) or admitted "older" adults as provisional, "high-risk" students only. Such policies deny evidence of continued intellectual capacities, particularly when opportunities for continued learning are available.

This is changing, as fewer young people are available to attend colleges; many schools have already observed that the expanding "market" of students consists of adults, particularly older adults. Courses can be arranged to meet their needs for technical and professional updating, life enrichment, or second-career preparation. Meeting times, course structure, and course content may have to be different than for late adolescent and young adult groups. For example, older adults do not do as well on rote memory learning (perhaps we should minimize that at *all* ages), and they may not as readily accept an authoritarian style of teaching. Most important, we need to reconceptualize education as continuing throughout life, and provide a range of opportunities to do so.

(4) *Reduce sexism.* Sexism, like agism, shapes our life chances, and the different value placed on male-female characteristics costs, financially and emotionally; it costs us as individuals and it costs us as a society in misdirected and underused talent. Reducing sexism and working for equality does *not* necessarily mean denying or destroying basic sex differences; it does mean that those differences are not automatically assumed to *in*clude people or *ex*clude people from particular jobs, incomes, educational opportunities, etc. For example, there is no reason that only men should be expected to lift heavy loads and run the risks of hernias and back trouble, or that women should be denied high-paying jobs because they require heavy work; each individual must assess his or her capacity and interest for the job.

Reducing sexism will make it easier to grow older. Women must become economically independent, so that they will not face old-age (and middle-age) poverty. Early socialization should emphasize preparing for a worker role. Household work and parenting must be recognized as work, with some kind of pension, if not pay. Women must not be dependent on the "good will" of a husband (or welfare) for support. Men should not be *assigned* the full financial burdens of family support.

Parenting must belong to both mother and father, and compensation should be allowed for caregiving. Many women now have low career achievement and little financial independence because they are assigned the job of caregiver. Both parents should decide how best to divide the care of children and the household, and employers should not interfere with such decisions. (Some companies refuse to hire a woman who wishes to pursue a career while her husband stays home to father.) Nor should custody of children go automatically to the mother. Both parents should have the option of retaining close ties with children, and looking forward to the sense of continuity that can come with grandchildren.

Sexual preference should be no basis for acceptability—as a worker, parent, student or friend. This should be a personal matter; women may prefer, for example, to live with other women as they grow older and few men survive. Male and female homosexuals should have equal rights to create happy lives throughout adulthood.

(5) **Reduce racism.** The costs of racism are similar to those of agism and sexism. Racism implies that some cultural styles are "better" than others, and that individual abilities differ on the basis of race. Racism in aging implies not only economic penalties for minority groups, but also a devaluation of one's life that may affect the final life review. It is more difficult for the powerless to age and die with dignity. Agism, sexism, and racism must be attacked on both a personal and institutionalized basis.

(6) **Make support systems a basic right** in an affluent society. Currently the availability of medical care, good housing, psychological services, education, and legal counsel is very unequal. Many of these services are used mostly by the poor (welfare pays) and the wealthy (who can afford the fees). The poor and the elderly receive help out of an ambivalent sense of charity; we alternate between presenting it as a human right, as a generous act by the competent, and as a payoff to remain out of sight and off our conscience.

Medical care is particularly important as we grow older. Medicare should be extended to cover all ages. The emphasis in medical care should be on prevention rather than merely on cure; this is less expensive in the long run and will maintain functioning longer.

Health-care delivery systems must be improved. This may mean reallocating authority within the medical-care team, since there are too few physicians and the structure is too hierarchical to provide the most effective health-care delivery. For example, the position of nurses should be upgraded, they should be paid commensurate with their responsibilities, and trained in the special health needs of older adults.

One of the special services needed is psychological counseling. It is clear that the changes which aging persons encounter are often stressful. We need more formal ways of getting help during these periods. This would be in the form of "transition counseling," as is now available for engaged couples and new parents. We need special places to go to talk about our options and our feelings when we lose a job at forty, or when a wife returns to work, a husband dies, or we move to a retirement hotel. These may be crisis interventions, coming to deal with a specific urgent problem. Of course, prevention is more desirable than cure. We need people available to listen to our responses to issues before they become crises. Such services are not envisioned as psychotherapy in the traditional sense of helping disturbed people. You don't have to be sick to get better.

We also need effective psychotherapy services. Given the evidence on the continuity of coping styles, we should deal early with destructive ways of confronting stress and change. Psychotherapy is far from being an exact science, but it has potentials for helping people cope better. Therapy should be available to persons of all ages. Most therapists have been biased against older people; they have seen them as being too rigid to change, and they may also fear dealing with the issues of aging because they are then confronted with their own mortality. However, there is evidence that therapy is effective with older adults. Age is not as important as intelligence, emotional flexibility, and desire to change.

A number of *community services* should be available to help maintain people in their homes—such as a visiting homemaker/friend who could run errands, tidy up, make a hot meal, mail a letter, visit, and refer the individual for further special services. Programs that bring one hot meal a day—and a friend to eat it with—have been very successful. All these are activities which individuals can do with little special training, but which are very important.

Housing needs are varied, and many forms should be available. Some elderly persons will want to live in apartments with central dining facilities, maid services, and "check up" services; some don't want to live alone because they fear having an accident or becoming ill and having no one discover their need for several days. Whatever the choice of housing, the rooms should allow for the retention of personal furniture and memorabilia. Housing arrangements must also allow for privacy and for meeting continued adult needs for intimacy. Courtship and sexuality should be a natural part of old age homes; current practices of segregating men and women (and sometimes even married couples) are inappropriate.

Some prefer communities designed for older adults; some want homes for the aged in a 'family' community. Some would prefer simply a day-care center, where they could receive some structure, stimulation, and food, but keep their own homes.

At some point, nursing home care may be necessary. The important factor is not to infantalize the residents. It is easy for the caregivers to assume that the elderly residents can do nothing, or that because they cannot walk they cannot hear or think. Most older people can maintain self-care functions, if they are expected to do so, given time to do so, and are in a humane, facilitating environment. The efforts should be on "normalizing" the environment and the residents, particularly in institutional settings; that is, the support services should be minimal to enable the residents to continue functioning as normally as possible. We can help caregivers in institutional settings accept the sensual needs of the residents; some perfume, flowers, a sensuous massage, attractive clothing can all help balance the loss of self that may accompany institutionalization.

Transportation services are particularly important to older people. As one gets older, it becomes more difficult to drive safely, particularly on high-speed highways; the difficulties are related to visual changes, and slowed responses. Good, safe, public transportation is necessary. Small changes can make even current systems more useful, such as easily read direction signs, and steps not too long and steep for arthritic legs. Younger people with cars can help by sharing their transportation with older people they know.

General environmental planning for older adults means not planning everything for the most agile, affluent members of society. Pedestrians should have walking rights-of-way, traffic lights should be of long enough duration to allow crossing time for the elderly, wheelchair ramps and bathroom facilities should be standard and universally available, and shopping should be available within walking distance.

You may wish to think about your own future—whether you might wish to live in an age-integrated community in which you could see the whole life cycle lived out. If so, we must create and sustain more of them.

We live in an exciting era. The future can be even more so, if we begin to plan for it now.

further readings

Atchley, Robert. 1972. *The Social Forces in Later Life: An Introduction to Social Gerontology.* (Belmont, Calif.: Wadsworth). Comprehensive, well-written, current introduction to the study of later life.

Brantl, Virginia and Sr. Marie Raymond Brown, editors. *Readings in Gerontology* (St. Louis: The C. U. Mosby Company, 1973). Good selection of readings on recent and relevant issues from the disciplines of gerontology, psychology, physiology, medical science, sociology, social work, genetics, and nutrition.

Cabot, Natalie Harris. 1961. *You Can't Count on Dying* (Boston: Houghton Mifflin, Inc.). An interesting, informal description of research on some 1,000 normal individuals over 50 who came to the Age Center in Boston.

Cowgill, Donald O. and Lowell D. Holmes, Editors. 1972. *Aging and Modernization* (New York: Appleton-Century-Crofts). A few highlights of a cross-cultural theory of aging are presented in this book; the book includes evidence from many cultures in order to sort out universal and culturally dependent factors in the status of the aged. Fascinating reading, and not terribly technical.

Davis, Richard, editor. 1973. *Aging: Prospects and Issues.* A monograph from the Ethel Percy Andrus Gerontology Center, University of Southern California, Los Angeles. Includes papers by authorities on various aspects of aging; aimed particularly at people working with older adults. Informative and well-written.

de Beauvoir, Simone. 1972. *The Coming of Age.* Translated by Patrick O'Brian. (New York: Putnam). Fascinating account of historical views of old age; unduly pessimistic view of current aging.

Eisdorfer, Carl and M. Powell Lawton, editors. 1973. *The Psychology of Adult Development and Aging* (Washington, D.C.: The American Psychological Association). Recent articles on gerontology as a field, experimental psychology, developmental processes, clinical psychology of old age, and the social environment of aging.

Goulet, L. R., and P. B. Baltes, editors. *Life-Span Developmental Psychology: Research and Theory* (New York: Academic Press, 1970).

Kimmel, Douglas C. 1974. *Adulthood and Aging: An Interdisciplinary, Developmental View*. (New York: John Wiley & Sons, Inc.). A good sequel to this book; includes eight "case histories" to illustrate points.

Le Shan, Eda. 1973. *The Wonderful Crisis of Middle Age: Some Personal Reflections* (New York: David McKay). A delightful look at the positive aspects of growing older.

Nesselroade, J. R. and H. W. Reese (Eds.). 1972. *Life Span Developmental Psychology: Methodology* (New York: Academic Press). Good resource for understanding and doing research.

Neugarten, B. L. 1968. *Middle Age and Aging: A Reader in Social Psychology* (Chicago: University of Chicago Press). 62 research articles on a variety of topics, with helpful editorial comments introducing each section.

Palmore, Erdman, editor. 1970. *Normal Aging: Reports from the Duke Longitudinal Study, 1955–1969*. (Durham, N.C.: Duke University Press). Reports on the first interdisciplinary longitudinal study of aging in our nation, carried out through the Duke Center for the Study of Aging.

Palmore, Erdman, editor. 1974. *Normal Aging II: Reports from the Duke Longitudinal Study, 1970–1973*.

Riley, M. W., A. Foner, and associates. 1968. *Aging and Society, Volume 1: An Inventory of Research Findings* (New York: Russell Sage Foundation). Invaluable source book; an organized encyclopedia of social research on middle-aged and older people.

Riley, M. W., M. Johnson, and A. Foner. 1972. *Aging and Society, Volume 3: A Sociology of Age Stratification* (New York: Russell Sage Foundation). Presents a model to describe social phenomena of aging using traditional sociological concepts; fairly technical but worthwhile.

The Gerontologist is a quarterly journal "for the professional who keeps abreast of new developments in the aging field" published by the Gerontological Society. Nontechnical, very interesting; often publishes special issues devoted to particular problems such as housing, minority patterns of aging, retirement, etc.

The Journal of Gerontology is a quarterly journal of scholarly articles published by the Gerontological Society. Subscriptions to this journal and to the *Gerontologist* are included with membership in the Gerontological Society. (Write to the Society, #1 Dupont Circle, Washington, D.C. 20036, for information on student, associate, or regular membership, or for subscription information.)

index

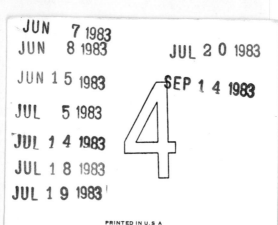